Darkness of Ego

KEVIN HUNTER

WARRIOR
OF LIGHT
PRESS
Los Angeles, California

Warrior Of Light Press
www.kevin-hunter.com

Body, Mind & Spirit/Spiritualism
Inspiration & Personal Growth
New Thought

PRODUCTION CREDITS:
Project Editor: James Szopo

Acknowledgements

Thank you to my spiritual posse that consists of God, my personal sports team of Angels, Guides, Archangels and Saints. Thank you, Saint Nathaniel, Luke, Enoch, Veronica, Matthew, Jeremiah, Samuel and Jacob.

Chapters

Author's Note

Darkness of Ego is another addition in the series of *Warrior of Light* books. The others include, *Warrior of Light: Messages from my Guides and Angels, Empowering Spirit Wisdom, Realm of the Wise One* and *Reaching for the Warrior Within*.

All *Warrior of Light* books are infused with practical messages and guidance that my Spirit team has taught and shared with me revolving around many different topics. The main goal is to fine tune your body, mind and soul. This improves humanity one person at a time. You are a Divine communicator and perfectly adjusted and capable of receiving messages from Heaven. This is for your benefit in order to live a happier, richer life. It is your individual responsibility to respect yourself and this planet while on your journey here.

The messages and information enclosed in this and all of the *Warrior of Light* books may be in my own words, but they do not come from me. They come from God, the Holy Spirit, my Spirit team of guides, angels and sometimes certain Archangels and Saints. I am merely the liaison or messenger in delivering and interpreting the intentions of what they wish to communicate. They love that I talk about them and share this stuff as it gets other people to work with them too!

There is one main hierarchy Saint who works with me leading the pack. His name is Nathaniel. He is often brutally truthful and forceful, as he does not mince words. There may be topics in this and my other books that might bother you or make you uncomfortable. He asks that you examine the underlying cause of this discomfort and come to terms with the fear attached. He cuts right to the heart of humanity without apology. I have learned quite a bit from him while adopting his ideology, which is Heaven's philosophy as a whole.

I am one with the Holy Spirit and have many Spirit Guides and Angels around me. As my connections to the other side grew to be daily over the course of my life, more of them joined in behind the others. I have often seen, sensed, heard and been privy to the dozens of magnificent lights that crowd around me on occasion.

If I use the word "He" when pertaining to God, this does not mean that I am advocating that he is a male. Simply replace the word, "He" with one you are comfortable using to identify God for you to be. This goes for any gender I use as examples. When I say, "spirit team", I am referring to a team of 'Guides and Angels'. The purpose of the *Warrior of Light* books is to empower and help you improve yourself, your life and humanity as a whole. It does not matter if you are a beginner or well versed in the subject matter. There may be something that reminds you of something you already know or something that you were unaware of. We all have much to share with one another, as we are all one in the end. This book and all of the *Warrior of Light* series of books contain information and directions on how to reach the place where you can be a fine tuned instrument to receive your own messages from your own Spirit team.

Some of my personal stories are infused and sprinkled in the books. This is in order for you to see how it works effectively for me. With some of my methods, I hope that you gain insight, knowledge or inspiration. It may prompt you to recall incidents where you were receiving heavenly messages in your own life. There are helpful ways that you can improve your existence and have a connection with Heaven throughout this book. Doing so will greatly transform yourself in all ways allowing you to attract wonderful circumstances at higher levels and live a happier more content life.

~ Kevin Hunter

INTRODUCTION

Saint Nathaniel and my Spirit team of Guides and Angels assist me in giving examples of how the ego in human souls cause so much unnecessary pain, destruction and loss in themselves and in others. This is done effortlessly through the direction of the human ego. We will barely scratch the surface since the ego is incredibly complex, but it would give one a basic idea of how and where the ego is indeed causing negative issues. We would understand that some of this would seem much like common sense, but we can also agree that if this were the case, then the world would put in effort to change it.

It is important to my Spirit team to address the state of humanity in this rather dark and bleak way. If the masses of human souls that inhabit the planet operated from the lighter side of their ego, there would be more love, joy and peace on Earth. The *Darkness of Ego* would not be necessary. The ego is a powerful force within every soul. Its goal is to associate itself with anything negatively based and expand it. This includes disruption, destruction, catastrophe, fear and paranoia. Any word aligned with negativity is delicious food for the ego.

My editor described the *Darkness of Ego* as being the darkest book I've done to date. He went as far as to say it was darker than *Paint the Silence*, which was a horror/action/drama book I wrote years ago surrounding a killer. If this book is considered far darker than a horror story revolving around a fictional vigilante slayer, then this should surely foreworn you of the tone that *Darkness of Ego* takes on.

There were moments I had a tough time writing this, let alone completing it and putting it in the can. Even after it was complete, I had it shelved for another couple of months delaying the release. The energy surrounding it was difficult and uncomfortable for me to absorb. Yet at the same time, it is content that my Spirit team of Guides and Angels urged me to discuss. It's wonderful to seek out avenues to improve your state of mind, and envelop your soul with the mantra of being all love and light. It's magnificent to put spiritual concepts into practice and discovering ways to reaching a happy place and living a stress free life. However, the reality is that what dominates the planet is an incredibly tense existence for most human souls if not many. These are concepts that need to be addressed and discussed, even if the right people who can benefit never see it. This is irrelevant, since the energy of this is out there in the universe. The title *Darkness of Ego* suggests that this is no ordinary sweetness and light spiritual book. Now that you've been warned, let's take a look at the little pest known as the ego.

~ Kevin Hunter

Darkness of Ego

CHAPTER ONE

The Ego

Every soul is on a spiritual path even if they're not a believer or follower of any particular denomination. They might not devotedly follow any belief systems, but they are still on a spiritual path. If your soul chooses not to follow any belief system with great discipline, then that is your belief system in this lifetime. If you're an atheist or agnostic, then that is your belief system. It is not uncommon for souls to evolve from one belief system to another while on their soul's path. These are souls who are searching for a higher meaning beyond what may feel like the mundane human physical existence. All souls are intended to gain necessary tools that expand and enhance ones consciousness while on their current path. The exceptions are those drowning in perpetual ego and selfishness. They are the lost ones refusing to believe they have anything to gain or have areas to improve on. It's much like being stuck in hardening mud until a circumstance comes about to knock you off kilter that assists you in looking at the bigger picture. It is the awakening moment where your higher self grabs hold of the reigns and smacks your ego and lower self out of the way.

There is always room for improvement. It's one of the reasons you're here in this Earthly school. You chose many of your experiences for your soul's growth. Perhaps you came into this lifetime battling a drug or alcohol addiction. Maybe you lost your parents when you were young, or you grew up in a difficult and challenging environment. Much of this is not by accident, while the rest of it is what the soul is attracting in while on its journey. This is based on the laws of attraction, energy and vibration.

The energy surrounding your feelings, emotions and mood you put out is what will be returned back to you. For example, you could mentally say something positive such as, "All of my dreams will come true." However, if the feeling you're experiencing behind those words is one of doubt or sadness that your dreams will *not* come true, then it is the feeling behind the positive words that will soon come into your world, rather than the actual words themselves. This is in the same way where you cannot tell a lie or get away with murder with those in the spirit world or heaven as your true feelings are always on grand display. It is important to watch your thoughts as it is to watch your moods and emotions. Keeping it all aligned positively and with great optimism is vital to your soul. This is the difference between what your higher self is ruling and what is your lower self or ego. Your ego will sabotage and coax you to feel pessimistic instead of optimistic. Your higher self is what guides you to a place where you're soaring high with joy, serenity, confidence and love.

Your soul is having human experiences for a higher incentive. If the reasons have not yet come to you, then you can be assured it will come to you at some point. This is either in this lifetime or after your soul has moved into the next room. Discovering this enlightening information is one that your higher self will assist in uncovering as part of your individual spiritual path. No one can point it out for you.

Heaven, God, the spirit world, your Guides and Angels will assist you in attracting in your dreams and keep you on the right path, but they also do not live your life for you. It's your life to live and no one else's. This is why they are called 'guides'. It is to *guide*, channel and steer you appropriately in a way that benefits your higher self's goal, but you make the ultimate choice or decision. This is where the ego comes in who will do everything, but listen to your higher self or any enlightened soul being in Heaven or the spirit world. If the ego is conducting your life, then it will do everything in its power to control and direct you down a darker path that is filled with misery, anger and negative circumstances. Your ego will cause you to second guess the nudges and messages your Spirit Guide and Guardian Angel are giving you. When you raise your vibration through positive life choices, then the communication line to your Spirit team on the other side is clearer. This is what leads you to a much calmer and peaceful life full of abundance and positive circumstances.

The biggest cause of turmoil and conflict in one's life is executed by the human ego. All souls have an ego whether living an earthly life or in the spirit world in another dimension. The most unruly and destructive ego that exists reside within every human soul on Earth. When the soul enters into a physical human body in the Earth's dimension and atmosphere, the ego immediately compresses and then swells up. It is the human souls higher self's goal to ensure it remains in check while living an Earthly life. The ego is what tests each soul along its journey. It is how one learns right from wrong. The experiences and challenges that the soul has while living an Earthly life contribute to the soul's growth. When a soul learns lessons, it is intended and expected to grow and enhance from the experience. Yet, there are a great many souls who do not learn lessons and remain in the same spot making the same mistakes over and over. The worst of the bunch are the ones wreaking all kinds of destruction and heartache in its wake. They operate from the most egos. They are asked to be re-born again into another Earthly life school in a far worse circumstance than the one they're currently in. This is for the benefit of teaching that soul some basic proper etiquette of behavior. Good people operate from horrid ego as well from time to time. It is common for those who are typically good people to be hit with challenging circumstances that test them by bringing out the dark shadows of their ego. Their basic human nature is good and they're able to effectively position themselves back into positive alignment. This is much different than someone who operates from nasty ego full time.

Many human souls have entered into a human life for the first time. They are known as a 'baby soul'. When the soul is birthed on the other side, it immediately moves into an Earthly life for its first class run. Earth life is essentially a school for these souls. This is similar to life on Earth where you are sent to grade school to hopefully learn how to be a functional and compassionate human being. As most have likely witnessed, this is not the case. What is taught are skills that one can eventually utilize in a human job of their choice, but that is where the teachings end. While this is an important component in gaining skill building qualities for that soul's growth, there are crucial elements that the human ego ignores. Compassion and love are two words lacking in teachings in the human school system. It is also lacking with the way parents raise their children. It's no wonder that Earth life is so chaotic, stressful and devastating. This lack of compassion and love has been present all throughout Earth's history, and yet it is the answer as to why you are here. It is what all souls subconsciously remember and desire.

Among the baby souls are souls who have lived an Earthly life before. They might be the ones who never gained specific knowledge or balanced out Karma from their hate filled wicked ways in another lifetime. They are asked to have another Earthly life after they've passed on. The soul mostly wants to have another Earthly life at some point. Their perspective on the other side is much clearer than when they were living in the Earth dimension.

Advanced souls in various levels of evolvement have also chosen to incarnate on Earth for important or specific purposes. One of them is in the role of teacher or leader type. This can be someone such as a compassionate spiritual healer, to an author or lecturer, to someone running important charity companies designed to help heal the world. Earthly life mirrors a school where you have students and teachers. The teachers enlighten these baby souls on the civil ways of functioning and behaving on Earth. You have good students and you have bad students just as you would in any human school on Earth. There are also teacher souls that incarnate into an Earthly life for the purpose of tempering the horrid negative energies which saturate the planet every second. The teacher souls are usually the ones who enact positive differences, changes, and benefits to Earthly life. Other souls are spiritual teachers whose role is to teach about love and compassion. There are teachers who might also be scientists, inventors, and even entertainers. These are the ones that positively contribute to bettering humanity through key areas such as bringing joy, love and compassion to others. Then you have the task mastering teachers who slap a soul away from bad behavior that will harm themselves or someone else.

The chaos, harm, and discomfort that have pervaded human nature for eons are executed by human ego. There is little light that exists in the ego, but there is some good that exists within the compartments of the ego. When you pull away the cobwebs, debris and dark fungus away from the blinding ego, glimpses of the light within the ego attempt to break out. Having a healthy self-esteem and drive to accomplish and succeed is the lighter side of the ego. Running others over in your wake to succeed is the dark side of the ego. It's crucial to identify, know and understand when the ego moves from the light into dark.

There is light within a healthy ego that reacts angrily to an important cause, but the anger comes from a place of love. For example, this is where one heatedly reacts with assertiveness towards an injustice or cruelty that was inflicted upon another living soul, animal or the planet. Although understandable to be infuriated when situations such as this take place, it is more so crucial that one tames the ego keeping it under much simmering control. This is by moving ones logical reaction from aggressive anger and into composed assertive diplomacy. There are different layers and levels as to which the ego operates from. For some it may move up and down into the varying shades of light and dark depending on what upsets it throughout any given day. While others perpetually reside in the dark side of ego, there are some who use very little ego and operate from the lighter shades of self-worth. They are easy to identify as these human souls are typically good natured loving souls who just want everyone to get along. They have a healthy self-esteem, which is good ego in action.

The ego is not something that a human soul can see via the human eye. Clairvoyantly it's no bigger than a pebble or kidney stone. It resides within the soul between the third eye and crown chakras. Not surprisingly it's black with a ring of yellow or orange tinge around it. This reminds me of what a Solar Eclipse looks like. The ego is invisible within the chemistry of the human brain. It's amazing that something so tiny can cause so much harm to oneself or in others beyond immeasurably large proportions.

It's no surprise that life on Earth is challenging and tough for so many human souls. These challenges are spearheaded by ones ego. Having an understanding of the basic functioning nature of the ego and the havoc it wreaks is essential as a human soul. We will touch on some of the predominant ways that the unhealthy ego destroys everything in its wake. It's greedy and wants to dominate. It is power hungry desiring to be number one at any cost. The ego sabotages that human soul and it's relationships through poor decision making. The ego destroys anything and everything that it can. The list of destructions and darkness it causes is endless. This is can be with circumstances surrounding relationships, jobs, humanity, nature, property, and people. There isn't anyone who has not witnessed the ego in action. It's especially impossible not to considering that it's in your face wherever you go. Every human soul is given an ego in order to test them for the benefit of their soul's growth. When you display a healthy ego, then you take two steps forward. When you showcase an unhealthy ego, then you take two steps back.

An unhealthy ego would be someone who criticizes someone who is doing well in the world. They would be a terrorist who murders another, to someone displaying road rage while driving a car because someone moved into their lane in front of them. Granted those two examples are vastly different ways the ego functions. A murdering terrorist is not the same as someone who displays road rage. Someone who displays road rage can essentially be a good person, but once their ego is provoked while behind the wheel you witness the monster in control. They're suddenly tailing the other person aggressively to intimidate and instill fear. This is the darkness of ego in action! Next the car ends up flipping over in the process causing a major accident. The ego has done its job, which is to see that soul make errors in judgment that cause a chaotic mess.

An unhealthy ego would bully an innocent person. A healthy ego is someone who believes in their talents and gifts to achieve and make magical manifestations happen. This type of high self esteem is the light of the ego. This is not to be confused with someone who treats people unkindly in order to reach the top and excel. This is someone consumed by greed and a type of grandiose self importance, which is the dark side of ego in action.

FROM THE AUTHOR

Over the course of my life I have been connecting and communicating with those in Heaven. This is not limited to myself or a gifted medium, since every soul that exists is communicating with the spirit world whether they're aware of it or not. When you raise your vibration and tune into your surroundings outside of the physical world, only then do you become privy to this communication. It wasn't difficult for me to know that there is more love that exists in any dimension, world or galaxy than on Earth. This is why I and millions of others incarnate into an Earthly life.

It is to be of service in a positive way. Training the masses who have very little to no love that exists within their hearts is no easy feat. They have allowed their surroundings and ego to govern their life full time while here, and that is no satisfying way to live. No one wants to know or be around someone like that.

Saint Nathaniel is a hierarchy spirit and one of my main guides. He sifts information, messages and guidance surrounding all things humanity through my crown chakra. He hails from the tribe of the Wise Ones on the other side. The Wise Ones have an ego, but it's not the same kind of human ego that governs them. Their ego typically shows up when no one is following their guidance or wisdom that is intended to help improve that soul. This is where they express some form of anger. The heavenly guidance they relay comes from their higher self and what others consider as God. Spirituality is not only living in the light, turning the other cheek, and pretending that all is okay. It is essential to remain in that loving space, but to also not be naïve to the dangerous waters that ego churns up. There is a darkness that pervades the planet and it is crucial in identifying its source. Targeting the ego's destruction on humanity is what's up in the next chapter.

Chapter Two

Humanity's Destruction

Why am I here? There's very little that's pleasant about this place. Oh wait, the natural wonders are magnificent and awe-inspiring. This includes the beaches, the deserts, mountains, and all of nature, but none of that is human created. The most blissful pleasant features on Earth formed at the planets conception. It is the reciprocated love between two souls in a committed union working together. It's walking through a garden paradise breathing in clear air and experiencing unadorned contentment. It's having radiant physical, emotional, mental health.

There are billions of human souls on Earth with one third of them called to duty to enact positive changes on the planet in desperate need of it. Every soul is assigned at least one Spirit Guide and one Guardian Angel who is with them from that person's human birth until human death. If the Earth's population is estimated to be around 7 billion and every one of those 7 billion people have two spirit guides with them, then that's 14 billion Spirit Guides and Guardian Angels in the different dimensions working away with that soul they've been assigned to. This is to give you a frame of reference as to how busy the spirit world actually is! Those beings are then working with other people's Guides and Angels to help them in a myriad of ways. Some will assist human souls in connecting in a love relationship, friendship, colleague setting or other purposes. This is with the goal that benefits the soul's growth in both individuals. Other times it is to assist the soul in reaching feelings of joy, peace and love. The angels know that when a human soul is in this original state, then they are able to attract in positive abundance. They are more apt to conquering their life purpose, helping others or the planet in a positive way. They do not enjoy seeing human souls experiencing misery and unhappiness. You can see how complicated this gets when you break down what they're all up to in the spirit world.

Human souls sit in jobs they hate to make money to spend on "things". This hard wired, materialistic, struggle is a product of programming from previous generations. Many want to see a positive shift in the world where peace reigns on all, but that's challenging to shift on a global scale. There are too many opposing sides and opinions with no happy medium or balance. It's that soul's way or the high way. The ego acts out in a tantrum fury on another soul who doesn't believe or follow the things they do. They often do this without having been asked for their opinion.

A stranger reads an internet comment they disagree with. This comment was posted on their social media account. The message or comment comes in the form of a negative, critical attack. The human ego wants to dominate and have power and control. This most primal way of reacting has been going on for centuries. It's barbaric, animalistic, and a poor use of time and energy. Human souls as a whole are unable to wrap its mind around the concept that this way of life serves no one. The human ego is to blame as it prefers to keep you and your higher self suppressed. One might be aware of this when it's pointed out, but it's quickly forgotten as they drudge on with their day-to-day activities. Human souls function like cattle due to societal programming. They are miniscule and insignificant from the grander perspective.

Human ego does not want to listen to a "know it all", because then it feels inferior or secondary. A well adjusted soul is not threatened by someone knowledgeable or one who owns there life. The ego is all about power therefore it denies guidance and wisdom that is intended to improve and enhance ones soul. The ego wants to be #1 and will not listen to ways it can progress. Its role is to push the human soul down and prompt them to act out negatively. It wants to sabotage that soul, which the human soul allows. Everyone wrestles with a nasty human ego, however those with an elevated consciousness, or who are spiritually evolving, use less of this human ego than say a criminal who has been tormenting and harming others in some form their entire life. The levels and the degrees of which others use the dark side of the ego are vast and complex.

The media and political arenas contribute to a great deal of the negativity that plagues the planet. It's typically the negative news stories that gets picked up and talked about through social media, news sites and water cooler circles. This is what gets spread like wildfire. News outlets are known for resorting to gossip instead of accurate reporting. What does this say? Humanity as a whole globally is not interested in anything good. They are lost in the thud of gossip and distraction. If something good is suddenly blasted and picked up around the world, there would be enough people to find something negative to say about it. This is the state of humanity. To not believe this is the case is to function in denial. It's not getting any better despite what some optimists might believe. If it were getting better, then the majority of the stories that would get picked up and spread around the world would be positive stories. Positive stories do not excite the human ego. Ones lower self receives a nice drug high from gossiping and turning everything in their lives into drama or negativity. This pushes the mass majority into feeling miserable and stressed out. They might have blips of enjoyment, but the overall unhappiness that exists within them shines through in what they perpetuate out into the media. They have not come to the conclusion that the way things are in this world do not work. There's nothing good about any of it. To be disconnected from anything outside of your self is detrimental to your soul.

Before the year 2000, journalists went out into the trenches to find a story. After the year 2000, as the Internet and social media took off, journalists rarely went out into the field to report on a story. They scoured the blogs and other less than news worthy websites that had a huge following and basically re-worded the information. It is more or less a cut and paste job to get the same news filtered out and as quickly as possible on any given day. Whether or not the original information reported is accurate or biased becomes an irrelevant factor. Fact checking is no longer on the list of requirements before posting a story. There is little to no journalistic integrity involved in reputable news sites. The real danger is the kinds of media hungry stories that are propelled out into the atmosphere from these sources. This is on the list of what has and continues to damage humanity. It feeds toxic energy out into the Earth's atmosphere that the lesser evolved would deny. There are those who succumb to the allure innocently and naively because it's all they were taught growing up to know. It is that soul's higher self's intention to break away from the monotony of media toxicity.

Gossip media is one of the many leading the pack. The reality is they stay in business because enough of the public's ego is transfixed on it. If there is no interest in something, then it will die off. This has not happened with the gossip media since too many human souls get their fix from it. This is predominant in the United States where celebrities are elevated to the status of royalty as if they are Kings and Queens.

Conduct a thorough examination process within you to discover what is missing in your life that would cause you to be driven by negative talk about someone. What influences dominated your life in adolescent years to grow attracted to gossip and negativity? There is no real reality when it comes to the media and gossip. All human souls will eventually reach this conclusion when they pass on, but why wait until that day? Have you asked yourself: *What is the point of my existence? This most certainly cannot be it. It has been pure drudgery fawning over what strangers are up to everyday. I need to attack them in order to feel better. I need this rush as my life feels pointless otherwise."*

You cannot watch trash television regularly and be that in tune with the other side. Negative entertainment in abundance is a block that prevents heavenly messages from sifting into your consciousness. The activities that you partake in, which include the media you read and watch, seeps into your perception often without realizing it. Therefore those that spend their daily lives watching reality TV or reading gossip sites regularly have the least heavenly spiritual connection with the other side. It is a dangerous, toxic addiction to be fixated on the superficial. A high vibrational soul might find themselves reading a negative story once in awhile, but this is about those who fall into its trap and remain there. It's a daily drug fix high to read it, gossip about it and comment on it. For the most part, a higher vibrational soul is turned off by negativity and typically avoids it like the plague.

News sources used to be balanced covering both sides of a story in an objective way. Now whoever runs the particular website or cable station is only interested in manipulating the truth so that it favors that company's personal views. This further divides humanity thus fueling the case of starting a culture war with one another. When these human souls have passed on, they will realize they put so much energy into something that is immaterial and without validity. The Internet gave voice to those who are in no position to have one. This is apparent on all comment boards that exist on news worthy and gossip sites. This is where the unpleasant side of humanity shines through.

This hyper technological world has damaged personal relationship connections. People discover the ugliness that lives within human souls through these avenues. They are not of love or God regardless of one's beliefs or lack of beliefs. It's 100% toxic and there is no room for any other kind of energy to grow beyond mold. The comment boards, forums, blogs, critical review pages and social media platforms attract more negativity than positive. It's instinctual and human nature to attack while hiding behind a computer screen. No one can physically harm you so you're free to be as nasty as you want to be.

Instead of writing one's thoughts in a diary on a matter, they want the world to know how much they hate a person or group of people featured in the media. It is a form of bullying and bullies act out of repressed rage beyond what they are truly upset about. Their ego needs to be stroked and they need to feel as if they're in a position of power, otherwise they'll have a tantrum. The negativity that exists in the comment boards and forums alone is a mirror of the ugliness that currently exists with human souls. They can pour out all of their repressed or damaged inner feelings out and no one can stop them. This stems from what they've been taught, from their upbringing and their peers. They easily believe this is the way, because they haven't been shown anything else. Comment boards should be banned as there is no real positive benefit to it. They are devices to hide behind a safety net and attack others. It is negative noisy energy that does nothing to help anyone.

FROM THE AUTHOR

Wise Ones, such as Saint Nathaniel, often have a harsh view that the end of times are near. Although this is a bleak view, their anger is due to the continuing destruction being enacted on Earth and its people. Careless human souls have been acting out on each other and the planet without any room to breathe. Someone gave you a beautiful home to live in for free and you're trashing it and each other. The end times might not be visible now, but if you notice the things such as climate changes, human disasters, and the rapid population increase that's taken over the globe, then one can see that this planet could very well reach a state of being inhabitable. This is also why there are many evolved souls being born into a human body to fight against this resistance and make necessary changes to improve humanity and the Earth's habitat so that this does not happen. Care about this planet and each other. Take action steps to improve it by leading through example. The odds are that if you have *Darkness of Ego* in your hands, then you likely already lead by example or are on your way.

CHAPTER THREE

Mass Hysteria and Spiritualism

The top baby makers continue to be those lacking in a primary elementary education and those living in poverty. They bring masses of Children they cannot afford into the world and resort to abusing them. The children end up homeless, unloved and without basic education. The wise tend to be more responsible when they have a child ensuring they are indeed evolved enough, strong enough, and with enough resources to raise a child. Those who do not hold those qualities have the baby anyway out of a selfish desire or through society's programming urging them that they must procreate. It is an egotistical decision to bring a child into conditions which are harmful and unrealistic for the raising of a child. If you do not make enough financially, then you should not be bringing a child into your environment. If you are emotionally unstable, then bringing a child into your surroundings is not wise. There are egos that believe it is what God wants - which is an untrue myth. There are over seven billion human souls all around the planet at this time. Human souls have procreated enough. They've created mass hysteria globally in the process. Many of those babies grow up uneducated and living in poverty as well. When they grow older, they repeat the same cycle multiplying at a dangerous rate. Only this time the reproduction of human souls is too great to control. They have not reached a full level of awareness to see the concept of this poor design, nor do they care. When someone cares, it shows through their actions and life choices. The ego is at the helms in these scenarios as it is more interested in riling itself up dramatically over petty issues rather than facing and correcting the real problems that exist within the confines of humanity.

There are wise human souls who have been brought up in poverty and without education. There are also great deals of privileged educated human souls who lack in love, compassion and common sense etiquette and intelligence. It is important to understand these are generalities and not specifics. Warriors of lights are being born into challenging conditions of poverty and a lack of education in the human school system. They are naturally connected with the soul, spirit and a higher purpose and cause. They are the rare breed breaking away from the cycles of being brought into a challenging environment. It is a smaller percentage compared to the overall number of people being pushed out into the world in horrid unlivable conditions. The souls gain essential qualities while in those circumstances, which they soon apply towards their life purpose.

There are more people in the world than ever in Earth's history. Newer souls entering an Earthly life are more evolved than the previous generations while purposely opting not to reproduce. The world will gradually notice a drop in the astronomical seven billion population number. This won't be evident until the year 2150 and beyond. One of the main issues is those below the poverty level line are the ones reproducing by the masses. Much of this is due to the rule of the ego, which prompts the soul to make poor life choices. This isn't a matter of scolding or pointing the finger as all souls are living an Earthly life for the purpose of growth, learning or teaching. The intent is to wake others up to the damage being created. Those who are a part of this design will never see these words. If they do, they will likely deny it, not understand it, or respond with insult. This would be an admission of guilt by the soul's ego. When you're in school and you make a healthy array of mistakes on a project or test, a good teacher likely writes on the paper: "See me." A teacher displays concern to discuss the errors made in order to correct them. It is for the student's benefit in the end. This same concept applies to the Earthly *Soul Life School System*. Only this school has a much greater impact since it lasts lifetime after lifetime and beyond.

One day far out in the distance, there will be no government in the United States. The White House will become a landmark museum for tourists in the later centuries. Anarchy began its rise in the late 1990's and into the 2000's just as the Internet and social media rose simultaneously. The Internet and social media gave birth to anarchy. The anarchy and lack of government will blow up into chaos down the line.

Many who are self-aware and in tune notice the signs of this happening currently in small bursts. The masses do not see it, because if they did they would make contributions to stop it. Change starts within every human soul. The change will not happen from a ruler, the government or President. You cannot change on a global scale without first opening up the minds within every individual soul.

The mass majority has set the way others must live. It is all about others succumbing, folding, and agreeing with that point of view. The ego stomps around screaming about what isn't being done for them and how unhappy it is. It is interested in being heard, supported, and loved. Ironically those are traits that come from within the higher self, yet the ego and lower self disconnects from the access of the higher self and searches outside of themselves to find it. You'll be searching forever until you discover this truth on your own.

Organized religion will diminish and move into the bare minimum as spiritualism rises. The future generations want peace and quiet. They will aim to conquer this goal over time. There is less anger, judgment and hate involved with someone who operates from a high vibration. Souls in the spirit world, different planes, and realms are standing in line to be born to usher in this change. Many of them are moving in the direction of unity more than ever in Earth's history. They are moving away from what they consider religious dogma. Instead - they remain open and connected to God or a higher power and force in a bigger way. Some of them are getting lost along the way by believing in nothing. This is that soul's particular spiritual path. There is and will be a rise in the upcoming souls who retain their spirit connection from the point of birth. They are able to do this through a diminished usage of the dark sides of their ego. They will remain believers in something grander than the human body. Many human souls want peace and love in the end. They are over the old, tired, argumentative, hate-filled, critical and violent ways. The latter has got humanity nowhere fast. You're still fighting for the same power and dominance you were fighting for centuries ago. Are you done with your tantrum yet?

There has been a shift taking place where advanced souls on the other side and from the various spirit realms are being born into a human body. They are easy to spot as they are highly connected to the other side. There are more being born now than ever in history. This is partly due to the massive outburst in population that has plagued the globe. When you have more people on the planet, then you need more soldiers of the light to counter balance this. The advanced souls that incarnate into an Earthly life have to drudge through a human experience with challenges that get in the way of their life purpose. Luckily, these souls will pick up on this inner calling that is connected to an improvement of humanity and the planet at some point in their human life. They are the ones who contribute to this positive shift of making the planet a more peaceful and harmonious place. Some do this through peaceful activism. While others shine their inner light on all those they come into contact with. Love is contagious and enough of it will stomp out the darkness on the planet.

When human souls are born, they are operating at top capacity. They are 100% connected, psychic, and in tune. That is until society, their peers, and surroundings quickly influence them. This causes an array of blocks which prevents the input of heavenly guidance and messages from reaching them. Since they are receiving no input or are unaware of where it's coming from, they come to the conclusion that they must indeed be alone. It is the belief that there is no afterlife, spirit world, Heaven or God, and all psychics are scams or frauds. This would mean they are a fraud since all human souls are born psychic. This is part of where the rise of Atheism or Agnostic beliefs has come out of. This was innocently picked up on during ones upbringing. While some have converted to a no belief system preceding a non-stop array of challenging circumstances that hit them. They might have grown up in a household where it was never discussed, or they asked for help and felt they received none. This is where faith comes in to empower you.

Science and spirituality should work together instead of trying to oppose one another. Opposing gets you nowhere. Being open to all possibilities gets you everywhere! Scoffing doubts are a lower energy and you do not want to remain in that space marinating in it for too long.

As spiritualism rises, religion moves into the bare minority. This is currently being seen as Churches attempt to attract in members. Other Church congregations are evolving and altering their services to be more open minded and inclusive of all people in order to bring in members. They are also seeing the love in all of God's creations instead of pushing the

Hell and Damnation card for all eternity. That was man-made superstition instructed to the masses during the deep dark ages when man was afraid of everything and full of fear of the unknown. To still be playing that card stunts your spiritual growth possibilities. Fearful superstition comes from the darkness of ego.

Human souls are finding out the answers for themselves. They are tuning in like they used to in centuries past. They will tune in more instead of relying on what their friends or peers are feeding them. As other souls move away from the hardcore religious establishments that have been more judgmental, the world will also see a decline in atheism. Atheism was birthed out of its Mother, which was hardcore religious dogma. It's ironic that one extreme side is responsible for creating another extreme side. Many who are atheist have admitted that their reason for becoming so was due to their upbringing and the harsh brainwashing at the hands of a religious fanatic. If this wasn't the case, it was by being fed this negative perception of religion by the dominating media. The unfortunate side to this was that both sides spawned out of some form of judgment and hate. This causes those blocks which prevents someone from remembering or being in touch with their true nature or something outside of themselves. There is no big man in the sky instructing orders that cause destruction to humankind. This is also not the end when your body has officially reached its current human death.

Being too extreme causes the most friction and unhappiness in human souls. With no room to breathe within the harsh confines of one's mind creates an array of walls difficult to scale. It's the biggest cause of anger, stress, hate, wars and hostility. This is by being too Democratic, too Republican, too evangelical, too atheist, too left wing, too right wing and the list goes on and on. Being too rigid and on one side of the fence doesn't bring people together, but rather separates them even more. It creates antagonism instead of peace. This is taught by the ego in one's peers, society and surroundings. It's not something that is developed on its own. You were not born rigid and unloving.

It is important to have room for movement and an understanding of others. Avoid forcing engrained harmful beliefs on those who are choosing a peaceful path. This is when someone volunteers information to someone that says that they're going to Hell. It's when a stranger takes it upon themselves to retaliate against someone for having a different opinion or belief system. It is against God's law to enforce and demand that someone follow your personal belief system. To angrily attempt to debunk something you do not believe in comes from the dark side of one's ego. There is no love or God for that matter in that space. Souls have been granted free will to choose how they wish to live their human life without interference from other human souls. This is in keeping that they are not harming or hurting themselves or someone else. The free will law causes so many mistakes in this world, but you are granted that freedom for a reason. You need to make mistakes to learn and grow your light.

There are human souls who have no real connection to the other side. Some have no belief in anything except making money. They're not living a life of joy, peace and harmony. They're working 9-6 jobs that are cutthroat. They are in their cars driving under stress with aggression nearly running over pedestrians and other cars. They're not extending kind words when someone does something nice for them. They are not saying thank you when someone holds the door open for them. They are miserable and unappreciative while deteriorating at a rapid pace without realizing it. It saddens Heaven to see this pain and loss of love in so many souls. The nature of how life on Earth has been designed by human souls has been constructed in a way that kills that soul gradually over time. Hostile human souls have risen to the surface. They are prevalent in great numbers unable to effectively navigate through the intensified energies. Human souls are the number one greatest contributors to unhappiness and misery in themselves and in those around them. Who else do you think is causing this? Someone's cat? God? No. The human soul's ego is to blame for the agony and suffering that exists.

Earth has unfriendly energy flying around in immeasurably dangerous ways. It makes you feel like you have to be on constant guard. You move about ready to fight off all those that come at you with their antagonistic energy. Perhaps you have the stance of always having to defend your territory from those that attempt to enter your vicinity without your permission. When this happens on a severe scale, Mother Mary says she comes into your life to say that this requires silence. She says when this happens it is a sign that you must disconnect and turn it off in all areas you are able to. Shut it down and go completely still and dark. Disappear and extricate yourself from anything hostile around you. Avoid getting involved with others if possible at that time. It's understood that you might have obligations in your life where you have to face others. This might be at your job or you have to go to the store where you know it will be crowded.

Mary urges for silence whenever and however possible in the cases of hostility. Escape to a quiet location if you can. This is preferably in nature or you can create a calming sanctuary at home. Take a break from returning calls from those where you know you'll have to absorb their negative energy. It's too burdening on your souls back to take it in day after day. The negative energy from others is that soul's ego acting out. It's best to steer clear of the line of their unnecessary fire. It's essential to disengage and disappear to gain perspective. This means disconnecting from world technology *(phones, computers, etc.)* Take a sabbatical or trip into nature. Go with a love interest or a friend you enjoy. Read a book!

If you question whether or not you are peaceful inside, then this cements that you're evolving more than you might believe. Being evolved is asking the tough questions. It's examining who you are and how you act and react. This is how one continues to grow. It's being able to take a good hard look at yourself from time to time. When you notice areas where you feel you need to make adjustments, then you take action and make those modifications. Someone who has not evolved stays relatively in the same place. They believe there is no room for improvement. It's always about them, their needs, and what everybody owes them or isn't doing for them.

Others have purposely placed themselves in neighborhoods where they knew it would be taxing on their equilibrium. This prompted them to question what they were doing. It also made some of them question their sanity. Eventually they left those areas once they realized the work they needed to do while there was complete. The role you agreed to take on when you came into an Earthly life is going to at times put you in a position where you will feel challenged. This includes circumstances such as being in neighborhoods that you would typically feel uncomfortable to be in.

How many more of God's Children must suffer until humanity wakes up and sees the light and error of their ways? The streets of many countries are attacked by the worst kind of demon and horror you can imagine. This is the same demon that has been destroying this planet for centuries. It is the one that lives within the mind of every individual called the ego. When it grabs holds of the steering wheel, then there is no telling of the destruction it will cause.

In Gaza, Children were killed, losing limbs, dragged in blood half alive and going hungry. While American children are lucky enough to be playing with "Lego's" or their cell phones, the Children in Gaza were playing on tanks or they're being used as human shields. While Palestinian Children pretend to be soldiers holding toy guns to reenact abductions. This is what human ego is teaching newer souls. It's a cycle that perpetuates going around in a circle with no real destination.

Mobs mock the deaths of these Children. They are allegedly doing this in the name of God. God would love to know which God they're talking about. God - the one true source of light creator calls them godless, inhumane, and not of His word, so who they are talking about? Heaven can use some illumination on this Godless God they speak of. Anyone who kills and harms with malicious intent is barbaric and will have a huge load of debt to pay back. This could not be wished on your worst enemy. It is someone with no conscious who seeks domination and power, which is not real reality. The terrorist group ISIS is a perfect example of the darkness of ego in action. While those affiliated with ISIS might believe they are acting out in the name of God, they are in fact acting out of the darkness of their own ego. God is all love and it is considered a sin to speak or act in any manner that is the opposite of love. Whether they are actually a terrorist group is debatable depending on who you converse with. The bottom line is that the heinous atrocities they commit on humanity are equal to that of a serial killer and not aligned with God. Humankind just came up with a fancier word for what they do such as terrorist. As it stands, ISIS is growing and will continue to expand and dominate for eons to come before they are overthrown and conquered.

A peaceful prayer:

"Dear God, thank you for ushering in your warrior angel soldiers to infiltrate your light into the ugliest heart in all men and women responsible for wreaking unrelenting and pointless havoc in others. Do whatever you need to do in order to bring this to a swift resolution of peace for all involved. You have full permission to bring in the big guns. Take your light and crack open and shatter the darkness that plagues those who know not what they do."

CHAPTER FOUR

The Power of the Mind

$\mathscr{I}$t is true that having the great relationship, career and home will not necessarily make you happy, but you might likely be happier. It's a human need to desire the basic materialistic necessities in this Earthly life. It's important to remember that genuine contentment comes from within. Focus on adjusting any ongoing upsetting feelings and thoughts inside you and then work your way out. Unsettling feelings are the ego mind creating something out of nothing. It restricts you from moving forward. You have the authority to free yourself of the prison that is formed by the power of your mind. Both your higher self and lower self are in constant struggle over who is to be the driver of your life. Often times your lower self or ego insists on dominating. It dictates and instructs you on how you will feel or react to something.

If your mind can create this restriction, then it has the power to undo it. The power of the mind can cause you unnecessary harm, but it can just as easily break the heavy chains that latch onto your soul. Your mind digs these holes to bury you in and stop you from progressing. It will do this by prompting you to reach for addictions and time wasters. It will do its best to lower your energy and mood. The false reality your lower self creates has the intention of stopping you from experiencing joy. Ignore that voice and choose to be free! Re-center and align your mind by taking some quiet time out. Do this preferably in nature where Spirits power is heavy and therefore the healing qualities more powerful. Avoid choosing to needlessly suffer. Wrestle your inner ego demon to the ground. Decide to stand in the power of your high and most magnificent self.

Why does it sometimes feel like a job to get happy? Your thoughts can either cause damage or bring in magical manifestations to you. Which would you like to have? The irony we notice is that it feels so easy for you to think about the things that you're upset about. Instead think about the things you appreciate and love more often. When you're angry or negatively critical, then this adds unnecessary burdens to your aura. Your ego passes it around to those around you bringing them down in the process. They do the same and so forth. You notice how unsafe this makes the planet as it creates an endless pay it forward domino effect.

This dangerous energy that comes from your thoughts expands destroying anything in its wake. You do this by running into other souls and complaining to them. You call up your friends or run into a close colleague and gossip about the negative happenings in your day and life. There is so much energy invested in placing hyper attention on the negative circumstances that you perceive to be throughout each day. The additional danger is that nothing good comes of it. Not only does it darken and lower your spirit vibration, but it also brings more of that negative stuff to you. You are manifesting that which you don't want simply by talking and thinking about it. You can be an innocent soul who puts in the work to keep their vibration high, but by watching or reading any negative media force fed upon you will lower your vibration.

Think happy thoughts, feel grateful, appreciative, and move into the zone of inner stillness. Your vibration will rise and you will manifest at higher levels. Suddenly you will notice everything going right. It's one good thing after another. For instance, you receive a check in the mail you weren't expecting. This is followed by obtaining a job you were dreaming about. You head on outside and take a walk basking in the wonders of your higher self and run smack into your new love soul mate. This soul mate is experiencing the same vibrational rush too since like attracts like.

One soul is plagued with negative thoughts and is terribly unhappy experiencing one hindrance after another. This person finds sudden aches and pains in their physical body that doesn't seem to go away. They're late for work, get a flat tire, and their love partner breaks up with them. This is all in the same week!

You have the power to bring in anything you desire through the positive utilization of your mind. The gifts of manifestation live within you. It starts with your thoughts. You have free will choice to choose how you are going to use those thoughts. This is followed by your feelings. When your thoughts and feelings are balanced, aligned, and radiating with optimism on an equal level, then positive circumstances enter your life. When your thoughts and feelings are negative, then the opposite effects take place.

You might say, "That person I'm attracted to and desire will never be attracted to someone like me. And I'll never get that job."

What do you think you're going to get out of that thinking process? No love mate and no job.

It is understood that as a human soul something will throw your day off. It will spiral you into a negative mood. The challenge is then to be conscious of this when it happens and pull right back out of that before those negative thoughts cause additional catastrophic events to happen. The real reality of what you are experiencing at that very moment that has thrown your life for a loop has no basis for being. It is not real in the way that your higher self and soul know it. You are here in a physical body at this time, but eventually that body will be no longer. The things you fret over cease to exist and yet your attitude still sticks until you realize the truth. Just because others have said that this is the way it must be, does not make it true. This is their reality and the one they choose to live in. If someone is unhappy with you because of who you are and the way you choose to live your life, then the odds are that they are unhappy with everyone and everything around them. This is not your soul's concern to fret over someone else's challenges by making it your own.

Chasing physical interests only pushes it that much further away from you. Those who have an understanding of certain spiritual practices may find from time to time that when things go wrong, they might affirm positive words in a harsh angry manner. "I am happy! I have everything I want! I love life!" You are saying it fuming and irritated. The vibration that is being directed out into the ethers is an angry and irate vibration. The energy darted out is the feeling and your intent. When you feel this angry, it is best not to state anything at all until you've relaxed and calmed down a bit. Cry out for assistance to your Spirit team of Guides and Angels, or whomever you feel most comfortable with. You can cry out: "Angels! Help!" You are immediately heard. If you're going to cry anything out in anger, then scream out for heavenly assistance, since that's the positive help that will be forthcoming. You may need to have patience for any intervention, but have faith that you are indeed heard and help is on its way. This is far more efficient than immediately crying out positive word affirmations in an angry manner. Since it is the tone and feeling behind them that resonate with the universe.

When you are angry or upset, give yourself permission to have a time out and sit alone away from others. Allow the angels to lift the negative thoughts and ugliness off your body. Visualize these eons being lifted high off your body and soul until they are nowhere near you. Take deep breathes in and exhale out any negativity and ugliness. Find a space of contentment and allow it room for your positive manifestations to take flight. Someone who displays high vibrational traits is a happy person. They feel immense joy and this is outwardly directed. They're optimistic and kind, which is not to be mistaken for weakness. On the contrary, they are strong, yet diplomatic and compassionate. They're calm and peaceful people who show love to others. They guard themselves from harsher energies that might surround them. God gave human souls an ego and free will to act how they please even if it sinks their spirit and lowers their vibration. It is up to the individual soul to discover that the way they've been operating has not been successful.

Communicating with your team of Guides and Angels is praying to God. The billions of prayers that come from human souls look like varying shades and sizes of lights being shot into the ethers. Clairvoyantly it may look like magical white light finger painting. When angels see the lights that come out of human souls during a prayer or affirmation, they see their true higher self banging around somewhere in that dense body they inhabit.

It doesn't matter if you're an atheist, or if you believe in God or whatever your beliefs are. It doesn't matter if you call it a prayer, or a positive affirmation or just a thought. It doesn't matter if you don't believe in any of it. Heaven has heard you the second a thought has entered your mind. You have put it out into the universe. Your thoughts are prayers and affirmations. All thoughts are heard including the good and the bad. Regardless of the nature of the thought, you will likely get it. The response to your request is matched to the vibration of the prayer or affirmation you are putting out into the universe. There is no set time frame on when your desire comes to fruition. You may get it tomorrow or in six months. If you believe in obtaining something with powerful intention, then you are heard. The stronger your intention is, and the good nature of this intention, the more likely it will come to fruition.

The rays of light darting out from individual souls are in varying shades of light and sizes due to the intention and vibration of that prayer. If someone is praying or saying a positive affirmation, but yet there is no feeling behind it, then the light being shot out is dim. You are heard, but the way the prayers and affirmations are answered is much like an assembly line. Say your request with positive, uplifting feeling behind it. It's possible you've grown frustrated and this energy vibration is picked up on in your prayer. Seeing no movement has caused your faith to be shaken over time. The tone behind your prayer or affirmation appears weak. The light of that prayer and affirmation is not seen as strong as others.

In the past, when I've cried out in frustration or anger demanding assistance with something, I miraculously see it come to fruition. The angels do not see your ego stomping around in a fury, but rather your intention. The reason my desire came to realization was it was seen that I wanted it with all of my heart and soul. The energy of the desire is so great that it was matched and returned right back to me. New born souls in a human body are left at the mercy with those older than them who do not always know any better. An adult can deal with life's repercussions better than a human child. A mother, father, parent, or guardian's prayer request for help with their child is therefore heard first. Sometimes caring for a child that needs assistance beyond what a human soul can help with results in a cry out for help. This is heard and responded to sooner than later. The bottom line is to watch the nature of your thoughts, feelings, affirmations and prayers. If you feel your faith is waning, or you're reaching the boiling point of throwing in the towel, ask Heaven to boost your faith and patience. Continue to ask daily if you're not seeing any movement. Some people ask for help once and then weeks later will say, "Well I asked, but nothing happened." It's important to continue to put that positive energy vibration out there regularly. You're also developing a connection with your Spirit team in Heaven. This is rather than only contacting them when you want help or need something.

When I've asked for heavenly assistance, I always get it. Sometimes it's right away and other times it's eventually down the line. I found through experimenting with prayers my entire life that they do help. After you've requested help, you must pay attention to the signs that are being given. When you're bathed in negative emotions, then that blocks your clarity from seeing how the assistance is coming. Express gratitude along with your desires. It's important to include appreciation with your communications with Heaven. Whenever I head down to the beach near where I live, I say blessings and gratitude. I do this silently every time I'm there. I do not take the gifts handed to me for granted.

Sometimes the answers you're looking for come in ways that you do not expect them to. Other times there is a delay as Heaven maneuvers certain pieces of the puzzle before what's needed to know is revealed. There are also the experiences you have to endure in order to reach enlightenment on your own. Never give up communicating with your Spirit team and God. Have patience and faith that the answers will be forthcoming even if it's not on that given day.

CHAPTER FIVE

Karmic Debt

𝒺very decision and choice you make daily, whether good or bad, has a consequence. As this energy is put out into the universe, you have set in motion what is to come to you in the following year. The life you're living now is a direct result of the actions you previously made often without realizing it. This action or thought energy is multiplied to the third power and beyond. This means that what is mirrored and directed back to you due to one small misguided deceptive action, decision, or thought, ends up being something that pulls you and your life down. Do the right thing and learn to make sound choices in your life. The Karmic energy associated with things such as thieving and deception is huge. Understand the repercussions that will come out of an unreliable choice in the end.

In the field of spirituality, there is the teaching of giving away your gifts with nothing in return analogy.

However, there needs to be an exchange of energy. There have been some who protest why psychic readers charge for their reads. The psychic reader is working and performing a job. They have bills to pay in this current modern day age, but there is the exchange of energy factor as well. You're giving someone goods in exchange for goods. This is a balanced energy. You find other avenues and ways to give freely at the same time without monetary payment.

The human souls who have incarnated from the Realm of the Wise One are a little odd walking to the beat of their individual drum. They do not typically fall into any of the boxes that one might associate someone who is spiritual to be. There are varying levels and different degrees in so many areas within the context and area of the spirituality genre. There's room for all of it in what everyone is contributing from within it. Part of the *Warrior of Light* meaning is that you will have to go to battle at times in correcting what needs to be righted. This is what my Spirit team has been instilling in me since human birth. With that come some issues naturally. It invites in unwanted antagonism and energies. It's nothing that a warrior cannot handle or ignore. They have a job to do and anything outside of that is noise.

A woman named Beverly had told me a story of how her Guides and Angels wanted her to get involved with a soul mate to work on karma from a past life. Beverly said that she understood the lesson meant to learn already. She did not feel the need to go through with the relationship. She explained that her Guides and Angels insisted this soul mate is her life partner and that she is contracted to help this soul mate in this lifetime.

My Spirit team immediately flagged a couple of spots with this inquiry. One of them is that your Guides and Angels will not insist that you connect with a soul mate you do not want. When it is your true life partner, there will rarely be any long term resistance or doubt. Any doubts entertained come from the ego which wants to sabotage you in taking any responsibility in improving a soul mate connection. If your guides and angels ask you to work on karma with a soul mate, then trust your guidance. Regardless if you see the lesson clearly, you agreed to work this out with this person before you entered a human life. If you do not, then you'll have to do it in a later lifetime. It will not evaporate, disappear and go away.

If the connection is abusive in some form, then that would be a reason to step away. Your Spirit team would not insist that you remain in a hostile situation. This is your ego talking as it revels in seeing you suffer. Working on your karma with a soul mate can include coming to a place of forgiveness for any slights this person or you have done to the other. If there are negative feelings you have within you about this person, then that will be applied to your karmic thread that needs to be resolved. It can also be that this particular soul mate needs to balance out karma with you. By you agreeing to the connection, you're allowing this person to have that opportunity to bring peaceful closure to your union. Peaceful closure is where you are both content and at peace with wrapping the relationship up.

When souls cross over, not all of them share the same space. Your soul travels over to the dimension and area your vibration is at. Only on Earth do you share the same space. Criminals or rulers such as Hitler and Hussein do not get a free pass in Heaven. They have to go through a rigorous review as they're crossing over. The laborious reviews occur en route through what is called the *back gate*. You are made to know what you had done to every single soul that you harmed. Imagine going through the feelings and thoughts of one soul you harmed. You are experiencing what that one soul went through at your hands. Now add the array of an infinite number of souls that were harmed by your hand. This is a grueling process to go through for human souls such as Hitler. You have to pay the karmic debt back, which results in more than one repeated lifetime. These are Earth lifetimes where you are put in situations that are less than stellar compared to your previous lives.

It is not difficult to see what one would incarnate back into a human life as. For example: An abusive, racist, white, slave owner in past history would incarnate for another Earth lifetime as an African American. This is in order to balance out that soul's Karma with the hopes or intention they would unite all races together since we are all one. The separation that exists is designed and ordered by human ego. It has nothing to do with the real reality in the spirit world.

Someone might have distaste for homosexuals. In a past life they assaulted and caused harm to anyone considered to be homosexual. They stirred up the masses with hate words about them. This has its own karmic retribution. What do you think they incarnate back into another life as? A homosexual. God will teach you to walk in another man's shoes by putting you in those shoes if it'll get your soul to experience compassion. Of course this doesn't necessarily mean that if someone came into this life as an African American or as a homosexual that it is due to karmic debt they owe their soul. These are merely examples of the possible ways it could go and has gone for some souls.

All soul's have much work to do while here. There are things you're working on within you. Perfection isn't demanded by Heaven. The anxiety of perfection comes from your ego. Heaven wants you to put in an effort and do the best you can, but to be kind and compassionate to yourself and others at the same time.

About 75% of human souls will do a repeat life. This is at least one repeat life, which will be less than the current one due to that souls' *Karmic debt* being so great. For example, Katherine is currently living a life that is well to do with money and abundance consistently flowing in, and yet she is horrible towards other people on a daily basis. She has built up karma due to being cruel to others around her. She will be asked to do a repeat life whereby the money she has in this life will be taken away. In the next life, she may live in squalor and poverty in a third world country.

This is why it's important to do the work now and become as a great a person as you can be now. Examine your life with a fine tooth comb. Give yourself the critique you find yourself giving to others. Catch yourself when you are destroying someone else's life in the many harmful measure of ways that exist. Be aware of everything that is happening outside of your physical body and your material needs. Be mindful when you are walking out on someone in a soul mate connection who is good to you.

Karmic debt is not resorted to the criminals of society. Even good souls build up karmic debt. It's almost impossible not to build up karmic debt because you're having relationships with other souls that have complicated emotions tied to it. This is where soul mates come in. You might have a tempestuous love relationship with someone where it ends badly. Years have flown by and you still have not forgiven this person. This is displayed in how you continue to speak ill of them or scoff when their name is brought up. In this case, you have built up karma. The karmic debt is not that you reincarnate in a horrible circumstance necessarily, but you typically reincarnate with that person repeatedly, one lifetime after another, until you are on even keel with their soul. Reincarnating on Earth is the choice of both souls.

Reincarnation is the belief that when your soul exits your body it immediately reincarnates into another lifetime. There is a time period that goes by before you reincarnate. You have the choice to do so or not. The newer Earth souls do reincarnate more than once. One Earth class isn't enough especially if that soul did not evolve or gain crucial knowledge in the first lifetime. There is a difference between reincarnation and incarnation. Reincarnation is the soul re-surfacing in a new Earthly life to balance out previous karmic debt. They will learn additional lessons that were not gained on the previous round. Whereas incarnation are the souls choosing to incarnate in order to contribute something positive towards humanity and the planet.

There is much talk and fascination about reincarnation and past lives in many circles. My Spirit team has said that knowing ones past life is not important. It's fun to know for entertainment purposes and out of curiosity, but most of the time it's withheld from your memory bank because it's considered unimportant. What matters is your current life. You have worries, stresses and concerns throughout your life. Can you imagine if you had these same worries about circumstances that happened to you in another life? This is why it's withheld from your memory bank. What would it be like if you recalled all of your past lives? You're upset and someone asks what you're upset about. You say, "Oh something I did in the 14th century still plagues my thoughts."

The only importance knowing your past life has is that it helps you heal major ongoing issues you're carrying and battling with in this lifetime. If you're someone who has spent their entire life focused on lack, then there can be a connection between that and a past life of yours. If you're always having love issues or you have trouble forgiving others, then there can be a connection that exists in one of your past lives pertained to that. This isn't to be confused with ones current upbringing where fear may have been instilled in you in this lifetime at the hands of someone else. It may have nothing to do with a past life. As it stands, human souls love to conjure up fear energy. Just log onto the internet and read the headlines of the latest news and gossip stories. The darkness of the ego is prevalent on every street corner.

CHAPTER SIX

Heaven's Gate

On the ancient book it talks about how people lived for hundreds of years during the beginning of Earth's conception. To get into a book that is popular and controversial in a measure of ways would prove exhausting. I can only relay messages that my own Spirit team passes through me and not what human society says or follows. There are some altered truths and some fictionalized accounts within the book due to the perception of society during that time in history. If it is clear at how easily led humankind is today, then it is understandable how even less evolved they were hundreds of years ago. Look at how the masses follow one another like cattle today. Notice how they rally together in lynch mobs to crucify others they disapprove of. This is evident in the media and in the comment boards online alone. Behavioral instincts are predictable in the way others follow one another. This is apparent in how human souls treat each other, which is often in every way, but kindness. Look at how they are on the playground growing up as children in grade school. See how some of them are within the confines of their own households. If this is the case today, then you can imagine what humankind was like centuries ago when a book like the Bible was being put together.

Back in historical times, human souls were more in tune to all things beyond. They spent a great amount of time outdoors in nature and amidst the fresh air. They did not have phones, cars, computers and all of the other electromagnet technological gadgets that prevent others from truly spending time with one another today. Being able to connect to someone today so quickly has its grand advantages, but what about the disadvantages? The radiation that exists in all of these devices and appliances is contributing to rapid health declines. Technological communication gadgets have caused decay in face to face connections that used to be long lasting. When you grow up in a world that trains you to receive gratification instantly, then you're going to experience some issues.

Anything having to do with fear, guilt, or low self esteem in the great book is mythology. Only a human ego would write something like that, especially during a superstitious patriarchal society. Women were not considered equal until far into the 20th Century.

Some of the truths are that people did live longer than they do today. How the Bible or historians have come to the rough estimated numbers on how long people were living would deem unfeasible considering that the Calendar had yet to be invented or perfected back then. Despite this, I have been shown that humankind did live longer than we are now. This is easy to grasp considering that humankind had not yet turned the planet into the ticking time bomb that it is today. The stresses that are placed upon humankind now have become largely unreal and too complicated to understand. These are stresses that did not exist at the beginning of time. They did not have mortgages and rents. Humankind has turned their needs into complications. They have created this mess and others are here to attempt to reverse and correct it.

When life was simpler centuries ago, humankind was outdoors in the fresh air and that air was breathable. They'd wake up as the sun rose every morning and head out into nature for the day. They were not confined to boxes all day long. This is the way they do now in cold lifeless offices with poor unhealthy lighting. Imagine the toll that will take on you. Envision the repercussions on your health and physical body after a couple of decades. When human souls leave their office at the end of the day, they race home in a box that is their car only to walk into another box, which is their home! The amount of time that humankind actually spends outdoors is limited compared to how it was centuries ago. You might race outside for a quick walk only to retreat back inside immediately. The diets and foods were not yet contaminated, processed, and pumped with every toxic chemical you can imagine. In the beginning of Earth's time, human souls were not consuming hot dogs, chips, and ice cream on a daily basis. It's likely not surprising that in the beginning of time humankind lived a lot longer.

Some human souls are placed in the back seat when they pass onto the next world. They are on hold in Heaven above. They do not go through the front gate where you are greeted by angels, but through the "back gate". These are the souls who were careless or inhumane. It's the place you move to in order to learn about forgiving yourself for harm you have caused others. It is where you make amends and choose to work on your soul to be a better person in the next life. This can take some time to come to fruition. Others who lived in the Light on Earth and contributed positively towards humanity grow small light wings.

The back gate is another tunnel of light that is more or less taking the long way around into Heaven. This route is typically reserved for those who caused a good chunk of damage to other people while on Earth. They have quite a bit to amend, review, and come to terms with. The length of this path depends on how much needs to be reviewed with that soul. This is to also prep them for the work that lies ahead in the spirit world. This process also includes restoring their soul beyond the human part of their ego which is still with them.

You are having an Earthly life to elevate your consciousness by opening up all of your senses which enables you to be a conduit of the light. Be aware of what's going on around you, but remain detached from any drama. Do your best to be in tune to your soul's higher self. Focus on the source of love that resides inside you. This light of fire and spark dims due to the influences that human souls are assaulted with regularly. This light never truly dies and is always accessible at the hands of your higher self. Avoid becoming lost in the fog that finding the light within you is difficult to locate. It exists and resides permanently within you. Crank up the volume of this light and allow it to wash over you in a baptism.

Your personal team of Guides and Angels know more about what's coming for you, than you do. They don't always share or reveal this because there are experiences you need to be enlightened about on your own. This is why they insist that you learn to trust them and know that all will be well in the end. They know that what might be currently going on in your life is for good reason. Nothing lasts forever, so patience must be practiced. Have fortitude and understanding that there is a plan. On the flip side, some effort on your part must be put in as well depending on what the circumstance is. For example, if someone is complaining they do not have any money and yet they're sitting around at home surfing the internet instead of being diligent about looking for work, well what do you think will transpire out of that? Your Guides and Angels meet you half way when you show that you are doing what you can to assist as well.

Human souls have destroyed and wreaked unforgivable havoc on Earth for centuries. They continue to function in chaos at an accelerated rate. Throwing Children into a room full of toys will inevitably bring on tantrums and power struggles. This ensues as the child's ego attempts to dominate and nab the toy of their choice before anybody else does. This is animalistic and often seen as innocent by the parent or guardian's ego of that child. Heaven knew this would be the case at the conception of Earth. A place was needed where new souls would go. It was known that it would be much like throwing Children into a school playground in hopes they all get along.

CHAPTER SEVEN

The Ego's War on Love

*H*uman souls crave contact and love from others, even if the hardened ego denies it. Those who prefer to be loners, independent or living in the middle of the woods with no one else around grew to be this way due to societal conditioning during their younger life's developmental years. Deep within the DNA of the soul's core, the soul desires a love companion. This is the case even if the love companion they crave is independent natured themselves. An independent minded loner would have a better chance of going the distance with someone who is similar in that respect. You do your thing, I'll do mine, and every now and then we do our thing together.

One might not call this a love companion, but a friend companion. It's still a love companion regardless of the title you give it. The nature of closeness you have with this person is irrelevant. Your one true long term soul mate this lifetime could be the same gender as you. You might be sexually attracted to someone of the opposite sex, and yet the love companion you choose to be around through the duration of your current Earthly life is of the same sex. This doesn't have anything to do with engaging in physical intimacy with this person. There are a great deal of love relationships between two people where they are with someone of the same gender, but do not engage in physical intimacy because sexually they're attracted to someone of the opposite sex. This is the same case with someone who might be attracted to the same sex, but their soul mate lifetime love is someone of the opposite sex. These cases are just as much a deeper higher love than any other physical relationship. This is someone you feel the most comfortable spending the rest of your current Earthly life with. Over time you come to the conclusion that the person you want to be with is this particular person.

Some might flinch confused believing that the one true soul mate intended for them is supposed to be someone they have a sexually, passionate, hot love relationship with. Yes, this soul mate can have those qualities with you, but this isn't always the case for many souls on Earth.

One of the bigger misconceptions about long term love relationships is that human souls have this misunderstood belief that if there is no sex with a love partner, then the relationship must be over or they're not with the right one. The angels say this myth couldn't be further from the truth in real reality. It is the ego demanding that relationships satisfy their insatiable needs. There is a great deal of soul mate love relationships where they experience a sexual drought.

It feels as if they're stuck in a rut and have become more like roommates or siblings. There is a block that prevents them from being able to adequately move into a regular sexual physical relationship with one another. This can be shifted when both partners discuss this issue openly and with compassion. They both agree to take steps and make effort to be more physically intimate with one another. This is in order for the partnership to thrive and grow. Your higher self's soul is open in all ways conceivable. This goes for physical intimacy with a love partner too!

The other case is there is no physical sexual intimacy with the soul mate if it's a love connection with a friend who is of a gender you're not sexually attracted to in your lifetime. In this sexually charged world, this is a difficult concept for modern day human souls to comprehend, but Earthly life is slow to evolve to a higher space where complex circumstances unseen are understood.

The majority of the current crop of souls has been trained by one another to have an attraction to social media drama stimuli. This is a distraction from the real reality of the soul, spirit, and the point of all existence. There is nothing wrong with social media pending it's not used for ego gratifying purposes or to harm others. Both lower your vibration and/or create an additional negative Karmic thread on your soul's path. The key is to have a healthy balance and dose of this non-reality and the deeper truth of why you are here. The secret to soul fulfillment and evolement is being aware. It's being open to knowledge of the unknown or what is often misunderstood. Causing harm to an innocent sends that energy out into the ethers and eventually comes back to hit you. The only difference is the harm is magnified to the tenth power causing one obstacle after another to take place in your life. If someone continues to bully an innocent, then they're setting up a lifetime of chaotic problems on their soul's path. They might not see it right away, but their soul will experience this justice at some point.

The ability to love, give love, and receive love are part of every soul's make up when it enters into an Earthly life. Human souls were not born unfriendly, greedy, angry and selfish. This is the human ego and lower self running the show. It is not ones higher self, which is pure love and compassion. When someone displays love, joy and compassion traits all at once without wanting anything in return, then you can be sure that at that moment they're operating from their higher self's space. You've likely encountered this type of person in your life that exudes those traits. They are infectious and brighten your world just by being in your vicinity. Wouldn't you rather be in that space full time, rather than in upset and stress? It is understood that you live in a world with tampering energies around you. If you live in a big, unfriendly city, then you likely know how difficult it can be to navigate through the tempestuous waters day after day with angry, rushed souls around you. The love is nowhere to be found and you feel this, but often so does the angry soul. They've hardened becoming jaded and unlovable to themselves and other human souls. Yet, deep down at their soul's core resides the love they were born with. Their ego has rendered it inaccessible caging it and sealing in the goodness. This is why there are souls experiencing an Earthly life for the specific purposes of awakening and opening the hearts of these hardened souls. They might be someone the hardened soul crosses paths with and is showered with love and kindness from this other soul in passing. It allows a few cracks of light to burst out of the hardened soul's heart chakra.

I offer some insight, guidance, and steps in working to get to a more centered, peaceful space in my big book, *Warrior of Light: Messages from my Guides and Angels*. It takes work to reach a state of serenity. Sometimes you will falter and lose your way. All souls are works in progress. This includes the teachers and leaders of the world. When you gain the tools necessary to pull yourself out of the ugliness, then it gets easier to do so in those moments when you waver.

Love relationships in modern day era have grown to become more than an effort to find and a struggle to keep. Since many human souls are governed ruthlessly by the external and the ego, this has played a huge part in the demise of loving relationships. In the United States alone, polls and stats are being revealed that slightly more than half of the population consider themselves to be single. This data isn't taken seriously by anyone, and neither is the tragic reality pointed out. This is a sad revelation that further demonstrates that humanity is not evolving as quickly as one would like to believe. It is ironic considering that love is the reason all souls are here. Obsessions center on needs, excess, and selfish satisfaction. This satiating need to sharpen in on external fixation was taught to others by the masses in the media, your peers and society. This progression continues to be recycled generation after generation. It's a strange kind of zombie like transfixed eeriness that hones in on all things greed, material or external. Some human souls attempt to receive this need for love through external sources such as social media adoration. This is not love, but ego. It is done innocently at times since this is a soul who simply craves love.

It is easy to hypnotize a baby soul more than any other. Baby souls are on Earth for their first Earthly life run. The angels see them as naïve and innocent. Other spirits see them as dangerous, causing the most hate, destruction, issues and drama around the world. The baby souls are all of those things combined. They are both naïve and destructive. They're easily influenced and succumb to the intoxication of the images being fed to them. This is done instead of diving deeper into pulling out their true higher self's soul. If this isn't the case, then the soul is terribly unhappy with some part of their life. They might be under stress and experiencing prolonged feelings of negativity.

Social media and phone apps have also contributed to the downfall of long term relationships. There are positive benefits to social media, but what are the benefits with phone apps? The lonely and bored typically log on to connect with preying predators looking for the next best thing, or to fill up the emptiness the ego created within. You are one in a long line of people that someone is sending the same messages to. The rise in phone apps to meet people is another avenue to come into contact with those in your vicinity. This has its benefits to a degree for those who are either temporarily single, living in a small town with little to no people, or for hooking up. This can be misconstrued as a broad generalization, but we're not speaking in specifics.

Through research, I've discovered most people ultimately use dating apps for the means of hooking up with you at some point. Phone apps are a way to meet people in your vicinity at the touch of your finger tips. This is an exciting and alluring way to hopefully meet additional people who you hope will become important in your life. The issue is that the ego is looking for instant gratification with many, instead of developing something meaningful and long lasting with one person. These avenues satisfy the ego, temporarily relieve boredom, and fulfill ravenous addictions.

Some of the common inquiries I receive from others are where they are dating someone new or already in a love relationship with them. It isn't long before they come to me with a discovery. They discover by "accident" that the person they're involved with is on a phone app. They express confusion and concern unsure whether or not to say something to their partner. They don't want to upset them or find out they're up to no good. Instead they hope they can trust their partner enough to assume they're just on the app for friends. Friends with a gender they are attracted to? Sure it's possible, but it would lead a rational soul to question it.

This further cements that most have already placed a negative stigma on the use of phone apps. There are good people wherever you go, including on a phone app. The flip side is that it can be a device for narcissism and addiction. You're logging on day after day hoping someone can fill the emptiness that resides within you. This soon lowers your vibration leaving you perpetually glum and dissatisfied. You're searching and searching for people to connect with on the app. What about the people you know in person? These are the ones who are already in your life. I've watched a great many throw that away only to log onto a phone dating app looking for new people to develop nothing with. It's a cycle that never ends. It's a cycle that never ends.

Relationships are colder than they've ever been in this modern day, yet somewhat backwards civilization. The hyper-technological world has contributed heavily to the demise of real human connections. The irony is the issues going on in the world are stemming from disconnect with one's true soul and higher self.

Before the rise in social media and phone apps, human souls took the connections they had seriously. Now they disregard them on a whim for the next best thing that pops up on their phone. Operating from ego, boredom, or loneliness ultimately lowers your vibration. One is craving instant stimulation from anyone around them. It doesn't matter who it is. Most on phone apps are ultimately looking for a one night stand. Some will cut the foreplay and come right out and tell you, while others will work you a little bit before dropping the bomb that they're deeply and crazy attracted to you. You feel loved for a brief moment that someone finds your photo or photos attractive. Eventually your banter between one another dissolves as this person has moved onto someone else they're chatting with and saying the same remote things to. It's a cycle that repeats itself as you log back on and continue this drill with the next victim wondering if any of these people could be 'the one'. If they're not attracted to you, it's rare that they would attempt to get to know you at all. Everything is externally based. Do I like how you appear before I engage with more than a hello?

Your soul longs for the kind of eternal gratifying stimulation that cannot be fulfilled through immediate indulgence. It's an addiction within the ego that one feeds in hopes of finding the one awesome love, friend, or one night stand. This tears down your soul thus lowering your vibration in the process. It's the search that crushes your soul.

I've reviewed many cases where love relationships fell apart. Both partners end up back on social media and the apps searching instead of working on the connection they had. One or both will say something like, "Well our relationship was great, but there was something missing." They'll make a variety of excuses that are fixable in the eyes of someone operating from their higher self. There is no perfect relationship and it will always seem as if something is missing no matter who you are with. This is how you learn important soul enhancing traits while with someone. You accept your partner's neurosis as they do with you.

The ego is strong in others and demands to have all of its needs met at once. This is a false reality that will leave the human soul perpetually dissatisfied. As you grow older and find yourself alone feeling even more abandoned, your mind sifts through the many options and choices of soul mates that entered your vicinity during the course of your life. There may be one soul mate in particular that your mind drifts over to from time to time. You'll wish you could do things differently with them, such as make it work and not throw in the towel. Human souls are intended to partner up with one another in soul mate relationships and companionships. This strengthens your souls by merging both your lights. You have that loving, supportive companionship through all of your years on Earth. You are the anchor for each other when things get tough. It helps to have that other half to make decisions with while granting them and yourself the space your soul also requires for clarity. When you partner with the right soul mate relationship dynamic, then you add balance to your life that keeps you from diving too far off into the deep end.

When you ultimately merge into a love relationship, then remember to love each other up often. Touch, hug, and cuddle with one another. The physical body hugging another physical body adds positive health benefits. Clairvoyantly one might see the aura light around both people hugging. The light in both souls merges and the colors of their aura shifts from a dark muddy color if they were stressed to brightening up. This is doubling the power and effects that the hug has. It releases Oxytocin in the brain and relaxes the soul. Tests have been conducted on hugging where they measure the blood pressure in someone who is stressed out. The blood pressure rises in the soul who is lacking of hugs. While the one receiving or giving a hug displays a drop in blood pressure preceding a stress event. Hug someone whenever you can and spread the love. You can hug a friend, a tree, and even animals. Although the hug of a love interest has a massive health benefit due to the high passion and love quotient between them.

CHAPTER EIGHT

Soul Connections

Of the important love relationship soul mate is to enter the picture for someone, then nothing is going to stop that person from connecting with you. This includes free will choice. Free will choice can delay the connection from happening, but it will not delay it forever. Your guides and angels team up with your soul mate's guides and angels to orchestrate the connection. Once the connection is made, there is little that can stop it from moving forward. You both immediately take notice. Anything that does stop it from moving forward is temporary. Sometimes how it happens is that you continue to bump into this person until you both finally lock eyes. From that point, nothing stops you from communicating. You both know this is it. Note we said *if* it is the big soul mate that is intended to be the life partner mate. There is a synchronicity set up taking place in order to bring two souls together.

Everyone has numerous soul mates sifting in and out of their vicinity during the course of their lives. In this case, this is the love soul mate marriage that you connect with who sticks with you through the duration of your Earthly life in a love connection. These are not the soul mate relationships that come in the guises of friendships, colleagues or short lived love relationships. Those are soul mates as well who you made a previous agreement with. This is in order to connect to them briefly for a specific purpose. This can be such as balancing previous karma with that soul. They might be an awakener for you to prepare you for the REAL lifelong soul mate relationship.

If your soul is not ready for the real deal and you have additional tools to gain, then you will have a short lived soul mate enter the picture before the long term one comes in. You may even have many short lived soul mate relationships for a good chunk of your life before you are with the long term mate. If you are thrown to the wolves prematurely with the long term mate immediately, then it may end unhappily. You will both likely incarnate relatively at the same time repeatedly until the connection is balanced.

There is no stopping any soul mate connection from happening. If it's not happening with someone, then they are likely not the intended big relationship soul mate. You will know they are the lifelong mate, because you end up together for most or the rest of your current Earthly life.

Long Distance Relationships

There is a belief that one's soul mate might be living in another state or country. Your Spirit team would not place your lifelong soul mate somewhere else when you live thousands of miles away. If that were the case, it would be orchestrated or foreseen by your Spirit team that one or the both of you are going to eventually move to the same city, state or country you live in relatively soon. This would be within one to five years after the meeting or initial connection contact takes place.

There are many cases where lifelong soul mates and especially twin flames have crossed paths with one another while not living in the same state or country. This is more common with the twin flame relationship. There would be key signs to look for if it is a twin flame. One of them is there would more than likely be an age difference of about ten years or more. The love intensity between the both of them continues on until the end of time. They have relatively similar natures and personality styles that are complimentary for the most part. They have the same values give or take. Of course there will be slight differences in all of these aspects, but when it comes to love relationships, they want the same thing. They both admit they're comfortable being around the other. It is rare to witness couples both desiring the exact same thing, so when you have it, then be sure to never take it for granted! The ego enjoys taking everything for granted especially in love relationships.

The soul mate or twin flame connection that is long distance ultimately brings both people to live in the same city. At least one of the partners makes it happen without hesitation by moving to the same city area as their soul mate or twin flame. This process happens naturally and without force. For example, one of the partners suddenly chimes up to say they're moving to the other one's city in three months.

There are exceptions where a long distance relationship soul mate connection works. To understand if you fall into this exception rule is that you would know without a doubt this person is your lifelong mate. You both know it and stop at nothing to make it happen. This would be where one or the both of you move to the same city after getting to know one another. You develop a healthy long distance friendship before it moves into love relationship territory. You're both smart about the way you're coming together, because there is a natural ease between you. This friendship could endure for a prolonged period of time at first before you become a love item.

A healthy long term long distance connection is one where there is no consistent drama, arguing, and issues throughout it. That would be a Karmic relationship, which would need to be dissolved as the lessons have been learned. The soul mate or twin flame partner who lives in another area is a blissful contact between you both where little to no trust issues arises. This would be rather difficult considering that trust is needed for a long distance connection. Most long distance relationships do not work unless both partners set up a system where they alternate visiting one another regularly. This can be at least once a month. Over time this puts strain on less stable connections with one or both of the partners. The trust factor in a long distance connection needs to be there naturally between the partners. Ultimately both parties in the duo have plans to live with one another or live in the same town fairly soon after connecting. Nothing stops them from making that happen. The pull between the two soul mates or twin flames is incredibly strong that it's near impossible for them to not make that happen. There is no second guessing when it comes to uniting in the same city for good. These are some of the signs on how to recognize what kind of connection one might have in a long distance relationship set up.

Is This Person My Soul Mate?

A common question asked is, "How do I know if the person I'm with is my soul mate?"

The instant answer is that if you have to ask, then it is probably not your soul mate. It may be one of your soul mates which sift in and out of your life, but not the lifelong love soul mate. You would not need to ask this question if it is.

The longer answer is that you will need patience to see how your connection with them plays out if you're questioning if they're the big soul mate. If the person you believe to be your soul mate has chosen to break away from your connection by ending it, then you're moving into iffy territory. The way your real life long soul mate connection will work is that nothing can stop you both from making a beeline to one another. The

There is great optimism in giving human souls the benefit of the doubt that they will carry this love they are born out of through the duration of their life. It is intended that the human ego will not drift too far astray. It is understood that catastrophe would be and is possible. Angel soldiers and souls on the other side stand in line to be born into a human body. They are the human souls contributing goodness for the betterment of humanity. Earth is a place God created where souls are sent for the purposes of learning, teaching, growth or to have a first life run as a human soul. The ones on Earth for the first time tend to have the most amount of ego. They are naïve and innocent in their actions through the eyes of the angels, but they will not get away with harming others for free. A debt must be paid back from their actions. This will be collected at some point for that particular soul. They are the ones that harm, hurt and hate with no care in the world.

soul connection draw is too strong and magnetic to break. Even if there is a temporary break, it does not last long because the soul connection is too strong where both mates know without a doubt that this is it for them. It's not a one-sided unrequited love. A case by case examination would need to be made as to why both partners are no longer together and yet they both hold deep attracting feelings for one another.

Attracting in the Same Types of Mates

The soul mate connections you make throughout the course of your life are vibrational matches to you. If you attracted in someone you are constantly unhappy with for a soul mate, then come to the realization that you attracted that person and their energy to you.

I often hear others protest, "Why do I keep on attracting the same type of lover to me!?"

In order to break from that cycle, you would need to take action steps in raising your vibration in order to attract in someone of a higher caliber. You can do this by shifting your perception and interests in life to something more positive. This takes work since human souls are innate and their basic nature stays relatively the same. The way an individual behaves is taught and learned through their upbringing and the society they live in.

Many find they go through several short term soul mate love connections that rarely have much lift off. This is to teach you important tools that prepare you for the right one. This also raises your vibration to the right ones vibration. If you do not learn from those short lived soul mate connections, then you will continue to attract in the same type of short lived soul mates to you. They are the class that preps you for the right one.

Being Too Rigid In Your Soul Mate Search

Someone is single and looking to date, but they have the unbending list of what they're looking for in a partner. Many of the qualities on that list are of the superficial variety, such as what this potential soul mate should look like and how tall they should be, etc. This is someone allowing their ego to paint an unrealistic picture of a potential soul mate that has been airbrushed in a magazine. Falling for someone easy on the eyes does not mean it will be a lasting long term relationship. It takes more than good looks to be a stable, loving partner. You will be on the hunt for a mate indefinitely until you release this inflexibility. This is not the only way those who fall into this category see things with such severity. Most of their choices in life are learned. It's all they know because it was all they allowed themselves to know. Anything beyond their backyard is unseen. While all human souls have certain values of what they'd like in a mate such as the person be spiritually based or not be a cigarette smoker. Rigid egotistical qualities would be that this mate must look like an Adonis model or kiss the ground you walk on daily.

While having a physical attraction to a potential partner is helpful, it will not be what keeps that person around you indefinitely. Many are guilty of it to an extent as it's what the media has shoved into the minds of human souls during the developmental stage. If the person is not tall with a tight body and six pack abs, then you will not give that person a second look. You're searching for the image of a mate who has been airbrushed and photo shopped up in a magazine. You're looking for someone who resembles the Prince or Princess that exists in popular animated fable love stories. No one stays looking that way forever no matter how well you take care of yourself. The fit people in the world eventually witness a decline in muscle and body mass as they age. Bodies are not designed to last, even though it is vital you take care of your body, mind and soul in all ways possible while you inhabit it. The truth is many human souls fall in love and end up in long term relationships with those they normally might've considered to not be their "type". They end up falling in love with that person and vice versa regardless. This is a true genuine soul attraction. It is the souls being drawn in and attracted to one another regardless that they're not what the media considers to be exceptionally perfect.

Will a Romantic Fling Delay the Connection with my Lifelong Soul Mate?

A brief romantic fling cannot create a hindrance in preventing your lifelong soul mate from entering the picture. Nothing can permanently stop the life partner that is intended to connect with you from doing so. If you're with someone in a mini-relationship or a fling, and then the one that you were intended to be with crosses paths with you, there is no way either of you will not notice. The pull between one another will be too strong.

Some have left marriages when they discovered they have met their one true soul mate. This is the case where they've left these relationship commitment connections for someone who ends up being their partner until they exit this lifetime. This is not the case where someone leaves their partner 'thinking' this new person is the one they're meant to be with and yet that falls apart too.

Where Is my Soul Mate?
I've Been Waiting Forever!

When you're content with you, your life, and where you're at, then the right love partner enters the picture. If you do not love yourself, how do you expect someone else to? I've witnessed others cry out in frustration that it's been years and no love relationship. It's the frustration energy that pushes the right person away. The right person isn't going to go after someone who has frustrated energy around them. This will turn off and repel the right one. Love yourself and be comfortable with being alone, while being open and receptive to what and who may come.

Having Endless Issues and Drama in your Current Relationship

When you are in a healthy relationship, it will not feel like you're pushing against resistance. If you feel that you run into a roadblock with your current partner at every turn, then accept that this is how it is right now with your current partner, or choose to distance yourself from this connection. Being conflicted will not help in strengthening a love connection. In order for a relationship to thrive, you must let it go. You cannot wait for someone to come around because the odds of that happening are slim. This is not said to let you down, but the angels will not give someone false hope either. They are all about two souls working it out together. If both souls do not put in an effort to make healthy changes within the relationship, then it is likely to stay as it is.

The Deeper Love of the Twin Flame

The Twin Flame is the highest and deepest form of a soul connection. Twin flames rarely incarnate at the same time, even though there appears to be a trend that many are searching for their other half twin flame soul. It is not the goal to find one's twin flame since they cannot be found. When it is time for a soul to connect with their twin flame while on its soul's journey, then it will happen naturally with no effort. This is similar to the image of magnet attracting in steel.

Most human soul's twin flames are on the other side. Searching for someone who is not living on the

Earth plane may result in prolonged disappointment. Every single soul knows their twin flame personally, even if they do not remember them while living an Earthly life. Your soul is part of their soul. Your souls split apart breaking into two when your soul was formed and sparked out of God. This is like human twins who have formed out of the same egg. With that come the many similarities and natures between them. Those who have a twin sibling mostly do not always look identical or have exactly the same interests. Your twin flame does not look like you, but there will be a great deal of similarities and a huge bond and attraction that never ceases throughout the course of your Earthly life. Remember it is not one sided as both of the twin flames feel this attraction and intensity for each other indefinitely. This is the case even if they temporarily separate or one of the partners flees out of a need for independence. Fleeing is common among a twin flame. Their ego will want to focus on more practical matters rather than succumbing to the depths of an intense love connection with someone.

On Earth, usually one or both of the twin flames are involved in positive spiritual or faith based pursuits. If one is more involved in it than the other, then the other soul will display growing signs that they're heading in that direction. They are likely the younger partner of the duo, but not always. This is a human soul who has evolved to the level greater than the superficiality of the physical world. This isn't to be mistaken with two people who are involved in religious pursuits which harm others through words or violence. The twin flame soul is highly evolved beyond hate filled dogma.

It is near impossible for twin flames not to merge together in a love relationship. It's too heartbreaking on both ends for them to be apart for too long after they've first connected. The twin flame connection can be a tough connection to bring together at times. Sadly some twin flames connections come together, break apart, come together and break apart and repeat. This is due to one or the both of their egos denying they're meant to be. One or the both of them may sabotage or pull away from the connection due to its intensity. Yet they manage to end up right back together months or even years later again. There's a cycle where they are two peas in a pod, then a period where they have little to no contact with another, only to be back in one another's arms years later. They wouldn't be able to function or continue on through life indefinitely without the other one. This is on both ends and not just with one of them. If it's just with one of them, then that's an unrequited love, karmic connection, or soul mate relationship.

There's nothing wrong with someone being a soul mate relationship over a twin flame. In fact, the soul mate connections are at times easier than a twin flame union. Soul mates experience friction as well, but twin flames are more intense and feeling oriented. This contributes to the additional difficulties. The friction with twin flames is in coming together. They have trouble connecting and sealing the deal. This friction is due to ego. Human souls grow uncomfortable or over emotional when feeling a heightened love attraction for someone who feels the same way about them. This goes beyond a physical attraction and into an unwavering deep soul attraction. The more insecure partner of the twin flame connection may end the relationship more than once. Sometimes this is to pursue selfish ego gratifying needs, yet their twin flame partner will always be on their mind, or will continue to surface in their mind indefinitely throughout their life.

Everyone is with their twin flame at some point on the other side before they incarnate on earth. Many souls come to Earth either as student or teacher. Earth is school and all human souls are in class. When you graduate, then you go back home where your twin flame is waiting. This is why it's rare for the twin flame to be on Earth when you are, because one of them is usually more evolved spiritually. If that's the case, there is no reason for them to incarnate into a human body, unless they agree to an Earthly life in the role of Teacher or Leader.

This would mean that if your twin flame has also incarnated into a human body, they have done so as student. The Twin Flame mix on Earth is either Teacher-Student or Teacher-Teacher. This is also why there is often an age difference between both Twin Flames who are in a human body, since a student might likely be younger, but not always. This is additional friction compounded onto the two souls. In Earth years they are in varying levels of human development that rub against each other uncomfortably, and sometimes even human generational gaps. The exceptions are if the younger soul is evolving rather quickly and maturely, while the older soul is tolerant and patient with the level the younger human soul is at.

As we stated, there is often an age gap between Twin Flames who have incarnated on Earth relatively at the same time. They might also be from different states in North America or they might be from different countries. Think of the image of the actor/activist couple, Brad Pitt and Angelina Jolie who are twelve years apart in age and from different states. They incarnated relatively at the same time for the humanitarian purposes and fights they do together outside of making movies. Although they have an age difference common amongst Twin Flames, they fall into the roles of Teacher-Teacher as well as Teacher-Student.

Write a Letter

Write a letter to your spirit team of guides and angels that includes what you're looking for in a partner. You may choose to include in this letter that the potential mate be physically attractive to you, but remain open minded to how this soul mate will appear. This can also work for career, health or anything else you desire. You're merely having a one on one dialogue with your spirit team. It doesn't matter if you hand write it or type it into an email and send it to yourself. What matters is the feeling and intention behind the letter.

Reading the letter to your Spirit team every day is not necessary. If reading the letter everyday to them gives you added optimism by partaking in that additional step, then that's fine too. It would be a personal preference, but not mandatory. Write the letter and then release it to Heaven. Those who enjoy cooking might pick up a cooking recipe, but then will start making slight changes to that recipe so that it works for them. This is the same concept as when you take on a suggested formula such as writing a letter to your Spirit team. Follow your gut on what feels right for you and trust that. Remember to step out of Heaven's way once you've released the request to them. There is no time limit on when a soul mate will be delivered. It can be weeks, months, and even years, but the point is to not lose hope. In the meantime, get into the fun and joy of your life with positive activities. This will help you shine with radiance, which attracts in potential soul mate interests shifting in and out of your vicinity.

CHAPTER NINE

Bring Back My Lover

$\mathcal{L}$ove issues are more frequent than ever before due to the heavy rule of ego in this materialistic externally based world. One of the biggest inquiries I receive surrounding love is that someone's lover abruptly leaves the relationship. This results in the one who was left to feel eternally dejected. The partner that was left desires heavenly intervention to bring them back together again. Heaven cannot force someone to act a certain way against their will. For some cases, they might plant the idea in that person's mind only if it will benefit both of the souls higher good. And if it is part of the agreement both soul's made prior to entering an Earthly life. There may be cases where you believe with all your heart that your relationship ended prematurely. This may be the case to your ego, but not to your ex-partner or your Guides and Angels.

Not all relationship connections are intended to last forever. It is not uncommon to have strong feelings for your partner after they've exited the relationship. Your mind goes through a whirlwind of feelings that include sadness, anger, and pride rejection. You miss the good times you had and love the security that the connection provided. You're left in a state of shock mulling it over in your mind repeatedly trying to understand how the breakup could happen. This causes confusion as you thought everything was fine in the relationship.

You reach out to anyone who will listen to your troubles surrounding it. This is with the hope that this person you're reaching out to will offer you answers that will bring your lover back to you. This can be from friends, strangers, colleagues, therapists to psychic readers. Inside you desire that they will all tell you that this is just a temporary break and you'll be back together before you know it. In some cases, this does happen of course, but not always.

I've been in those love connections in the past where it was bliss without any major issues or arguments and it ended only to be rekindled again years later. I've also witnessed the red flags in other people's relationship connections, which both partners were blind to seeing. The person who was left in a relationship is in a state of shock. They are unable to admit the red flags were indeed present if they examine the connection trajectory more closely. You ignore the red flags when you're in love. If you notice the red flags, you think the person will change only to later discover they've ultimately left you in turmoil and heartache.

If you were left in a relationship by someone you deeply loved, then request heavenly assistance from your Spirit team. Ask that they help re-kindle the spark lost between you and your ex mate. If your Spirit team sees that the relationship is indeed over and has run its course, then add that they help you heal and move on. If they intervene to assist your lover to come back to you, this doesn't mean that person will acknowledge the heavenly guidance and nudges. Many do not listen to their Guides and Angels due to the over consumption of the ego and material world around them. The exception is a spiritually minded partner, but a spiritually minded partner likely would not have left their mate in the first place unless they were abusive in some form or bathed in addictions. Another exception is that the partner is moving into a period of soul searching and discovering who they are. They require space for a major transition. However, a spiritually minded partner more than likely would've discussed the break up with you so that you are both at peace with the splitting up.

The soul mate you love has left you and chosen to pull away. They distanced themselves from your connection for a myriad of reasons. You anxiously wonder and obsess if your lover will come back to you. You believe you received signs that they're interested in you regardless that they left. The angels know if a couple has what it takes to re-unite and make it work, but they cannot intervene with the other person's free will. If someone bailed out of the relationship, they do so out of free will and ego. This is powerful beyond any kind of heavenly intervention. It is important to note this since I have had others say they've asked

Heaven or their Guides for help in re-uniting them with their ex in a love relationship, yet months have passed by and there has been no movement or sign of it happening.

Heaven does not have control over how someone chooses to respond or not respond to your affections. The person you desire will show how they feel about you through their actions. Believe them when they show this. They might be unresponsive to your affections after the break up. When someone is interested, they will let it be known. When you reach out to someone you have interest in to see if they have interest in you, then do it with the knowledge they might not give you the response you crave, if any response at all. Prepare yourself for this and accept any outcome. This person made a decision to extricate themselves from your connection. This doesn't necessarily mean you did anything to cause that, which is something else that may plague your thoughts. You're likely to go through deep self-analysis to see where you might have played a part in the crumbling of the union. Sometimes you'll see where you made mistakes. Other times the breakup doesn't have anything to do with what you did or did not do.

Friends may urge you to move on and immediately see other people. Feel whole and complete within before you venture out into the dating field. This is another side effect after someone has left you in a relationship. You understandably want to get over it and move on as quickly as possible. This isn't fair to someone new when you're not ready and still have deep thoughts lingering over your previous partner. Understand the lessons that have been learned in the connection that ended abruptly. If the connection was submerged in red flags, unhappiness, or abuse, then in the future make a pact to only accept soul mate relationships that are loving and supportive. These are ones that enrich and nourish you, while you give this same support in return. Refuse to be part of any drama with a soul mate that makes you feel less than others. Aim to be around people whose lives are working. Choose to be around those who are making positive contributions. Be around those who are growing, evolving, and making soul contact. Sometimes you need to release soul mates because they are harmful in toxic ways you might not have been noticing, either to themselves or towards you.

There will be times when your ego has a difficult time letting go of an ex. You have loving memories of the good times you had with them. The ego refuses to believe that the connection and lessons with them are over. You wait and hope for that small glimmer of hope that there will be some reuniting taking place one day. Meanwhile, years have passed and there's been no movement. What will it take to see that the connection is indeed over? Sure there are cases where there is a reuniting that takes place in order to complete unfinished business, but those are rare cases. Incidentally, I have personally had that happen where one of my soul mates and I re-united years later and moved into a love relationship. The relationship was stronger the second time around. Regardless, it is vital to move on and start living again. Get back into the joy of your life. If someone is meant to be with you including your ex, then the re-kindling will happen naturally on divine timing.

I never advise that someone wait for someone who left them, no matter how big the feelings are. An exception would be if you have both discussed that you're taking a break or one of you needs your space. If you wait around hopeful that your ex will return, then this can create a block from allowing someone new from coming in to an extent. It becomes difficult for a new person to enter the picture unless it is the lifelong marriage soul mate. A sensitive person or the kind of love mate you desire will sense an ex's energy around you even if they're not aware of it. It's in your aura. When you pine over someone no longer with you, then your body language may slump more than usual without knowing it. Your energy may be suppressed showing signs of a prolonged disappointment with something in your life. This energy you're giving off is not conducive to attracting in a new love partner. You have to move on with your life. If your ex comes back one day to mend your connection, then great! If not, at least you'll be living.

It saddens the angels to see so many struggling in love relationships today. You were involved with someone romantically, only to have them pull out of your connection unexpectedly. One day everything seems like it was going great and the next day you get a message out of the blue that they lost interest. You wonder how it was easy for them to pull out or how they sleep at night. It's almost as if a light switch was turned off and they were no longer interested in a relationship with you. You were kind, compassionate, and loyal to this person. You attempt to make sense of it and wonder what you did wrong. You grow angry feeling like they wasted your time. You might find it difficult to pull through each day. Meanwhile, you know they've gone on and they're busy with their life as if what they did had zero effect on you.

If someone pulled out in this manner, it's likely they were already entertaining the idea of leaving you for some time, but putting on the face that all is well beforehand. If they were merely looking to pull out a month before they did out of the blue, then this is a behavioral pattern with them where they pull out of everything with a snap of a finger. It's not someone you would want to engage in a long term relationship with anyway. It is a form of deception and having deceptive energy in a relationship is not healthy for a long term relationship. You may have bit the bullet with this connection. Treasure the great time and experiences you had with your ex. Make your peace with it and let it go. This will lift your vibration which will help attract in someone awesome!

CHAPTER TEN

Getting Over an Ex-Lover

$\mathcal{Y}$ou've come to the realization that your ex who left you has indeed moved on. It's been months or even longer and there has been zero communication. They've either moved away or ended up in a love relationship with someone else. You now know that it is over. Coming to this reality might be painful, but it is also freeing on your soul as well. When someone leaves you, then you do not need to go through it alone. You will be tempted to email, text, and call this person with upset emotions. Some do the 'drunk dial'. The guidance is that you leave it alone. Nine times out of ten when you do reach out to them upset it has a tendency to back fire or blow up in your face. You come at your ex with heavy emotion and distress. Your ex is turned off and repelled by this energy. When you have no feelings for someone and they come at you with heavy emotions of anger and upset, the human instinct is to immediately display annoyance and anger.

Although, if it's someone you truly love, then you want to talk it over with them. This is another clue that the person that left has lost interest at that time. Knowing this information is helpful as much as it feels like someone is killing you.

Write what you want to say to your ex-lover in an email or letter, but do not send it to them. Send it to yourself or a trusted friend who understands. Lashing out at the ex will not cause a dent except push them further away. They've already made the decision to walk away from you. They are not going to care much about how the split has upset you or what you have to say. They have absolved themselves of any responsibility with you.

I've received cases where someone wants to send their ex this letter. It should only be done when you know for sure that you are finished with them. Most of the time I've discovered that they're really only sending the letter in hopes of eliciting a positive response from their ex. Immediately the next day I will hear them say that there was no response to what they sent, or that it backfired with the ex telling them to leave them alone.

Why are you questioning that there is no response from your message to them? You sent the letter releasing the pain off your chest knowing that you're officially walking away. This letter does not contain anything positive, but is merely a recounting of all the times this ex hurt you. There is some colorful foul language sprinkled in it for good measure. Then they end the letter with, "If you still want to talk and work this out I'm available." This will not prompt the ex to grow a conscious.

You will need to work on getting through each day. Pre-occupy yourself with positive activities and healthy distractions as much as possible. Get to the space where you are feeling joy again. The depressing feelings surrounding your ex will be less hurtful as time progresses. It will be difficult at first as you push yourself to go to the gym when it's typically an easy occurrence for you. You just want to stay in bed or lie on the floor and not move. You grin and bear it. You pray and ask for heavenly assistance everyday and you keep going.

Let go of the why's, how's, and I don't understands. Make your peace with the connection dissolving. There will be no way to wrap your mind around it no matter how you look at it and dissect it to death. You have to allow yourself to move through each of the stages of emotions such as sadness, depression, then anger and resentment. Eventually this is followed by a transformation where you reach a place of peace and forgiveness for yourself and for your ex love. This is where you accept that this is the path your ex chose and you respect that. You do not need to take any responsibility for their actions. Thank them for the time you had together. Forgive them for your soul's benefit and then let the energy surrounding them go. There is no timeline for these emotions to work themselves out, but reaching the place where you're completely content again is the goal. It is where you can think of them and it is no longer painful. You discover they're with someone new and that does not bother you. Any difficult emotions experienced do more damage to you than anyone else. No one is worth that kind of pain.

Avoid remaining in contact with your ex when possible. When you have heightened love feelings for your ex and you were the one who was left, then this can be taxing on your psyche. You never truly move through the various stages of emotions in order to start living again. You find you're getting used to moving on in life without them, then suddenly they surface with a text hello and you're right back where you started. The love feelings come up again. You grow hopeful that perhaps because they're remaining in touch there is a possibility of rekindling the love connection. Whenever your ex reaches out to you it prolongs the pain. You'll be afraid to let them go and avoid contact because you do love them. However, know that constantly engaging with them when you have deep feelings for them can confuse you into believing there is still hope with them. That is until you discover they have added the '*in a relationship*' with someone else status on their social media account. You'll know when it's safe to form a friendship with them if this is what you both choose. It'll be the moment where your ex is with a new love interest and that does not bother you in the slightest.

When experiencing heartache over a love interest leaving you, then call upon Archangel Raphael and Archangel Azrael. Ask to be infused with healing love energy daily until you discover you've indeed moved on. The thoughts of your ex no longer bring you any pain or emotional discomfort. This means that you are no longer affected by posts they put up on social media, or when you receive that random text hello from them. You'll know when it's safe to form a friendship with your ex if this is what you both choose. It'll be the moment where your ex is with a new love interest and that does not bother you on any negative level.

When praying and asking for help, understand that sometimes your Spirit team will not always bring you what you want if they feel it is not going to benefit your higher self in the long run. They know what's to come up ahead and what you must endure. You might profusely request help and ask that a particular soul mate contacts you, but it does not come to fruition. There are a couple of factors that would prevent that from happening. The ex's free will choice. Consider also that your Spirit team is blocking it from happening at that time for your own soul's benefit. The answers as to when it will happen cannot be understood until time has passed. This is when all will be revealed.

Ask yourself the serious questions as to how you wish to proceed from this point on. Soul mates come and go in your life. Not all soul mates are intended to stay no matter how much of a huge impact they've had on you. Ask yourself the tough questions such as: "Is the soul work with my ex indeed done? If so, how long will I allow this breakup prevent me from moving forward?"

It's not uncommon for some human souls to have that great love they will never forget. For some it can be their first love. It can be the one they had when they were younger before they grew older and became more jaded to love. Perhaps it happened later in life. Fear keeps people in relationships that are long over. They're too comfortable and afraid to make a drastic change by walking away from a connection they've been unhappy in for years. Change is disruptive to human souls. If you do not change toxic situations, then you'll remain miserable!

It can be difficult for some souls to emotionally detach from someone they were intimate with for a long period of time. Most human souls do not automatically switch to being friends after a serious love relationship ends. The brief connections they had which only lasted a month or two can merge into a friendship with no problem. This is because you're not emotionally attached to them. The long term relationships are another story where there was a stronger long term bond. If you have deep emotions over a love connection that only lasted one to three months, then take caution with future love potentials. Avoid wearing your heart on your sleeve so soon with someone you do not know.

Having to put on the face day after day is exhausting as you attempt to get over an ex. You still have to go to work or the grocery store. You're inevitably going to see and bump into people depending on where you live. It is okay to give yourself permission to not engage with anybody unless necessary. The hurt and pain will come and go. Sometimes you'll be fine and other times you won't be, but over time it will diminish. Just keep moving forward and take it day to day. It's normal to have confused emotional reactions to someone else's behavior following a breakup.

Those who pull out of a love connection with someone they love might be seen as being in a state of self-centeredness, or going through a selfish period. Sometimes this is the case, but other times it's not. It's easy for the ego to grow angry when a lover leaves them. It's important to also consider that this ex-lover discovered while in a relationship with you that it is not what they desire. They might long to be free and thought they could do the 'relationship thing', only to discover it's not for them. Or perhaps they have some soul searching to do that requires they leave the relationship. Everyone is on their own soul path. It's crucial to step away from the tantrums of your ego and respect that.

There are souls who indeed have a pattern of using others in a love relationship. They might be the ones who do not have a history of successful long term relationships. They have a history of being in short lived connections only to grow bored and leave most of them sooner than later. They are living in the moment and thinking of themselves. They are not in touch with how their actions might affect someone else. If they do know and do not care, then that would make them a sociopath. Sociopaths do not have deep emotions for others. Selfish would be a more appropriate word. Selfish people do not change overnight. Learning to be selfless takes quite a bit of time. The selfish individual needs to want to become more selfless, but it's difficult for their ego to convince them that this is what indeed needs to happen. The selfish person is not out to get you, but they are thinking of themselves first. This becomes a bigger problem when it negatively affects those around the selfish person. The selfish person is too selfish to notice that their behavior is affecting others around them. Never wait for a selfish person to suddenly grow a conscious if it's never been part of their nature. In hindsight, if you examined the red flags in this type of connection, then you might see the signs that your connection would not last to begin with. You likely brushed it off until this person really did something awful to your heart.

While in the dating process, pre-screen your potential soul mates entering the picture. This way you can get a feel for the kinds of relationships this person has been in and what they desire in a love relationship. Dates that are serious about you tend to ask: "How long was your longest relationship?" If the answer is three months, well, I think you have your probable answer as to how it's likely going to go. When your love relationship ends, remain strong and pre-occupy yourself with fun activities, even if you have moments where tears form. Do not put too much pressure on your soul. You deserve respect from those you have shown love to.

Nothing is ever final even if it feels that way. Your ego wants to convince you that the despair is real. It is real in the way that your human soul knows it to be real, but it's not real in the grand long term sense. Allow your soul to breathe by moving swiftly through the traumatic experience. Moments of hurt will twinge your side from time to time. You might mask that with an addiction. While other times you'll push yourself to go to the gym. I've felt this kind of pain when it comes to a deep, loving relationship split. In my previous life, I found that I had a habit of attracting in soul mates that were living in the moment. They love you today, but tomorrow they likely will not. This is giving your power away to someone you put faith into. You realize they are flawed and have issues as we all do, but the issues they wrestle with have nothing to do with you. Unfortunately, sometimes it is at the expense of others.

Everyone's lives are constantly changing and altering. Nothing stays the same even if one wanted it to. The ending of a deep love relationship feels like a death. Your views and life take on an entirely new turn. Someone loses their job they thought they would be at forever. Their life is altered by that one act. They have to make plans they otherwise would not have.

Perhaps months have passed and you're still battling cutting the cords with your ex. If you believe your connection with them is worth saving, then reach out for one last bit of hope. The odds of them coming around and initiating a move could be slim. At least if time has passed, the heated emotions might have subsided with you and your ex. You might be able to communicate peacefully. If you do reach out to them, do it knowing that you might not get the response you're hoping for or they might not have any romantic interest in you. However, you will have your definite answer depending on the way your ex has responded. This can give you peace of mind that it may be time to cut the cords from the attachment to this soul mate for good. This way you are not stalling your soul from experiencing prosperous new connections. If your energy is heavily invested in this ex soul mate, then this can deter a new suitor who is trying to enter the picture. Someone who is high vibrational can sense an ex energy in someone.

A relationship break up puts you at a cross roads in attempting to forge on with or without them. You come to the realization that you need to make a choice. Will you hang on to your ex's essence in the hopes that there is still that possibility? Or will you open the door a crack for someone amazing and more aligned with you to enter the picture? This would be someone new who genuinely has an attraction and feelings for you. They're facing the same direction as you and value long term committed relationships. Even if you do move forward, it does not mean that this ex soul mate and you cannot become a romantic item at a later date, but until then at least you'll be out there living!

CHAPTER ELEVEN

Masculine and Feminine Energies

All souls have both masculine and feminine traits and energy within them. When you exude one trait over the other, then you create an imbalance that can eventually lead to complications or challenges. This is the same with giving and receiving gestures, which are both masculine and feminine energy. This doesn't have anything to do with what gender someone identifies themselves to be in this lifetime.

Masculine energy is external. It is about giving, action, security and protection. It's putting outward energy into something or someone. It can be promoting yourself and your work. It can be putting effort into a relationship.

Feminine energy is internal. It's about receiving, nurturing and caring. It's being open, compassionate and receptive. It is kindly accepting praise, compliments or monetary payment for your work. It can be accepting gifts of any type graciously from spirit.

It's receiving love with joy from your significant other and showing compassion for them.

Selfish and self-centered behavior isn't masculine or feminine at all, but one's ego and lower self. If there is too much of either a masculine or feminine energy trait in someone, then the scales tip creating an imbalance in your world. An imbalance blocks the flow of positive abundance to you.

Keys to successful relationships sustaining the distance beyond basic attraction, compatibility, and values are balancing these giving and receiving energies. A successful couple is happiest when they exude both masculine and feminine traits. This is regardless of the genders involved in that relationship.

If you have two love partners who are both "yang energy", or both "yin energy", then issues can arise. It helps when one is more yang (masculine) and one is more yin (feminine), yet at the same time both know how to incorporate an efficient amount of masculine and feminine traits. This applies to all couples regardless of their sexual orientation or gender.

American men have the stigma of being previously trained not to show emotional vulnerability. It was insisted by society that they behave in ways that are considered all masculine traits. Their life expectancy ended up being shorter than women since withholding emotion can cause health issues later in life. Now it's become more on an equal footing where the life expectancy for both is relatively similar. This has become less common over the newer and future generations of souls. The younger generations of men display and express more emotion and feeling, than the generations of long past. This is creating a more optimum balance within the composites of many men. In fact, there is more emotion in younger men than younger women. Some European countries and other cultures never had the odd stigma of how a man needs to behave and how a woman needs to be. They are more evolved in that respect.

Everyone has the masculine and feminine traits within them. The traits are perfectly balanced when you are born into an Earthly life. Once society, your peers, and communities get a hold of you with the wretched ego domination, then they can cause future issues within you that can be difficult to reverse. This is through human ego tampering. Other human souls insist on how you must behave and live your life. They ingrain it into your psyche on what activities you must partake in. This luckily shifts when your soul leaves the Earth plane and crosses over into the next room. Your soul is restored to optimum levels before human tampering entered the equation. This is why it's important to be focused as much as possible now. Avoid falling into the trap of believing what society and your peers say you must do or how you must act. Refrain from following the herd just because everyone else is doing it. Avoid being influenced by gossip and negativity. Just because a large percentage of people follow and believe that something needs to be a certain way, it doesn't mean it's true. You are a fully fledged thinking human soul and have an accurate barometer within you on what is right for you.

CHAPTER TWELVE

The Four Day Work Week

When you work 40 hours 5 days a week, you are working more than what you factor in. If you include the time you wake up, to getting ready, to jumping in the car to sit in traffic, plus that required lunch hour, then this is well over 40 hours a week. It is time to change the five day work week to four day work weeks all around the world. The current regimen adds stress, builds up diseases, and destroys the spirit quicker over time. This is not why your soul is here. It is one thing to do meaningful work, but to punch in and out at a regular job you don't care much about five days a week lowers your vibration and crushes your soul. Human souls are not robots and need more regular time outs. They require regular periods of fresh air, exercise, and nature outings to stay healthy and strong. This allows you more time to put towards your life purpose, as well as positive family and friend time. It affords you luxuries which are essential to your overall health and well being. This also gives you more time to make the real changes that need to happen on this planet and with each other. This is a critical topic because more people than not spend most of their life at a job. This has greater impact than you would believe especially with the working class. Heaven applauds hard work and rarely rewards slackers. You're not a loafer if you're working 40-60 hours a week and desire time to decompress.

Why do human souls break their backs five days a week? The majority of the countries around the world observe working 40 hours a week. This is typically 9 hours a day and five days a week. This does not include commute and travel time. For some, their commute can average 30-60 minutes and much longer for others. Everyone sits in their little boxes on wheels barely moving. They trudge slowly to their jobs all at the same time and then they all leave roughly at the same time in an assembly line. When you arrive back home at the end of the day, you self medicate with a beer, glass of wine, or something harder to decompress. The next day you repeat this mundane cycle hardening your aura in the process. Human souls adopted an absurd work schedule. Stresses build up permanently causing all sorts of complications as you grow older. It is time to put a stop to this illogical routine. If humanity cares about the well being of each other, then this would be apparent in the current functioning chaos.

Corporate greed has the most egos when it comes to the work week set up. They have been trained to make money-money-money! There is nothing wrong with making money to ensure you have a comfortable level of security to survive on this planet. There is something wrong with breaking your back for a good chunk of your life in order to do that. When you retire you're too weary to do anything and enjoy all of this money you made. Most who have spent their lives focused solely on making money have found they make less of it as they grow older. By the time they're on their death bed, they are near bankrupt or have less money than when they started. Once you pass into the next world all of the material items you gained stay on Earth. You do not take it or anything with you. Your clothes and mansion are left behind. Those you leave your assets and estate to will run through the money carelessly. When they pass on to the next life themselves, those assets will still be left. You also have to factor in that a corporation such as a bank hasn't repossessed or foreclosed what you spent a good chunk of your life building.

When you cut down work schedules to a four day work week, then you add benefits that pay off in ways that profit your soul. You have more time to recuperate and re-center. You have more time for positive human connections and interactions with loved ones, family members and friends. You have more time to exercise and take care of your body and soul that will extend your life expectancy beyond measure. It will cut back on all of the diseases and heart attacks that kill millions of people on a regular basis. It will cut back on human addictions with drugs, alcohol and food. It will cut back on the depression and unhappiness that plagues the world. You will have more energy and time to not only enjoy your life, but it will raise your vibration to a higher level. This enables you to be more in tune with your Spirit team. They assist you along a path that will bring you the happiness you crave while guiding you to make sound choices. This higher vibration prompts you to be extra productive and energetic. When you are radiant and full of energy, then the work at your job is dynamic and on the mark. Corporations and supervisors benefit because they have employees who are happier, full of life, and therefore industrious. This is evident in their work which helps the businesses they work for grow and prosper. Everybody gains!

Thirty to forty hours a week can be compounded into a four day work week. Having been in the work force for decades I can tell you that the odds of anything of importance happening on a Friday are rare. The majority of people working a five day work week are far less productive on a Friday than any other day of the week. Businesses are paying employees to go in on Friday's for no reason. However, there are many employers that release their employee's early or mid-day on Friday's. They are the businesses who know the reality of keeping one's life balanced. Many of these employers release their employees early on Friday, or they leave the day as optional to go into the office. This leaves the other businesses where the employees are not granted this luxury to basically sit around all day with nothing going on. The exceptions are retail businesses or companies that do not observe the standard Monday thru Friday - nine hours a day work week.

People are burned out by the time Friday rolls around. They're fatigued in general due to the buildup of this way of life. It shows when others ride the elevators to their offices and at least one person will say, "Thank God it's Friday." This is what human souls have become. To spend every week hoping that Friday comes along quick enough so that you can breathe! When the weekend rolls around, or your two days off is present, then you're still running around trying to get things done you were too exhausted to do the rest of the week.

When early morning Monday rolls around, employees move back into work exhausted. They grumble to themselves or those around them at how much they hate their job which equates to hating their life. You're spending most of your time at this job. Morale is low within all of these souls and companies. Others fear losing their job or are afraid to leave their job. They are tired, bitter and angry. This causes them to make more mistakes than usual. Their brains are not functioning at a high capacity. All of this blocks Heavenly communication and messages, which spawns the abuse of toxic addictions.

There is a huge crop of non-believers of anything outside of themselves. How can one believe in anything outside of themselves if they are consumed with material and greed? This over technological world has caused an array of issues in the way it's trained the current crop of human souls. Most cannot construct a proper email to someone else. These are professionals who display coldness in the way they work. Coldness does not equal money. Formality causes others to distance themselves from you. You're not personable, but repelling in that state.

Fewer souls are finding romance in this modern day world, and the ones that do find love rarely last. How can you attract in romance when you move through life aloof, sour, and fatigued?

People are too burned out to exercise. There are those who do exercise after work as if their life depended on it. This is great to exercise and it helps in decreasing the potential onslaught of health issues and diseases that can plague your body. There are those who head to the gym to try and keep their body in shape and look desirable. It's difficult to do this when you've been sitting in an office chair all day long five days a week. You move from your office chair to sitting in your car for another hour. You arrive back home to cook dinner and sit down for another length of time to eat. By then it's about 9 or 10:00 at night and you park it right on the sofa or your bed. You're too exhausted to do anything. Instead you count down the days until you have another day off. This is no way to live! The majority of the working class world would agree with the four day work week. Those who do not like that idea are usually the greedy ego driven.

Many employers are not working 9-6 shifts Monday through Friday day in and day out. Some roll in around 11 or noon or whenever they feel like it. They leave their offices around 4 or 5 or whenever they feel like it. The rebuttal would say, "Yeah, but they are a business owner and they can do whatever they like." This is true, but it doesn't have to be this way. Greed is moving out the door! The old ways of living do not work anymore and it's time to change.

Why not offer your employees a flexible four day work week that benefits you as a business owner. It can be broken up to a Monday thru Thursday work week or a Tuesday thru Friday work week depending on what the company is offering. This will also cut back on commute time, traffic issues and not to mention the abundant amount of pollution that is filtered into the air due to car and bus emissions being spewed out into the air full time. Naturally this is pending that when people are off work they're not immediately roaming around in their cars going somewhere they do not need to be going.

There are a great many jobs that can be done from home, but the company or corporation insists that their employees work in the office from 9-6. This is done in order for them to monitor their employees, even though some may cite that they feel that having that face to face interaction is the way to go.

A great employer will offer flexibility to their staff. This might be one that includes the employee working full time, but one of the days the employee works from home. This is pending that they have the kind of job where they can do it from anywhere. Some may feel that their employees will take advantage of this, but if you have a lack of trust with your employees, what does that say about your business? Working from home requires that you are on call or available in the event of an emergency. The bottom line is there are flexible ways that employers can instill a higher level of morale. They'll witness signs of boosts in energy levels in their staff by offering options to them. The work shifts used to be 9-5, before they expanded it to 9-6. The reason was to include a lunch hour. It is catastrophic to the well being of humanity when the egos in Earth's history chose to extend the work schedule for as long as they could make it. This decision is ego driven and made out of greed. It isn't someone who cares about the long term health and well-being of humanity. It's all about making money and increasing your bank account. Paper will eventually evaporate when you've passed on.

These unrealistic work week schedules have been in place for decades and nothing has been done to improve it. In fact, they've been worsened as evident in the extension of the 9-5 modification to a 9-6 or even 9-7 schedule. It is the role of many Warrior of Light's to make it known that it is time for global change in the work force. Incidentally, in my research I discovered that one of the top spiritually based book publishing houses actually offers the four day work week to their employees. This is no surprise considering that most spiritually based souls are indeed ahead of their time!

Employees leave work early when they can or when the boss takes off. They put in requests to run late for doctors and dentist appointments, car work and family stuff. This would reduce this from happening during regular business hours if the employee was working a four day work week. This would also cut back on the insaneness of weekend traffic when the entire world is heading to shop at the same time. Traffic on weekends is now no different than traffic on weekdays, except now it's all day long! When the world is working a four day work week, not everyone is going to be rushing out to go shopping at the same time. It'll be sporadic throughout the weekend, rather than on Saturday and Sunday afternoon when they typically tend to do it.

There are members of Congress who are absurdly trying to bring part time employees from a 30 hour a week employment to a 40 hour a week employment. They feel they are doing the employee a justice so that the employee can qualify for benefits. This is a step in the wrong direction. Why not pass measures and bills to alter the full time work week to include anyone working 30-40 hours a week. Divide the hours into a four day work week if necessary. In my investigations on this, when asked, more people have said that they would rather work longer days for four days if it means having a three day weekend. These work week rules are man-made and man-made rules are rarely stable in truth. No one does anything about this because it doesn't occur to them to do so. It's kind of like, "Eh, it's just the way it is." It's all they know. It's the rules. It's what everyone was taught. Taught by whom? Things don't happen unless you make them happen. Rules have changed over the centuries and they will continue to do so. One of the many fights my Spirit team has instructed for humanity includes the human soul work week dilemma. These fights are in place due to the massive improvement in bringing human souls more peace and joy in their lives. Everybody benefits including that soul.

Chapter Thirteen

Psychic Insights

*H*eaven and the Spirit World have an aerial of view of the trajectory of your life. They tell me that if human souls could see what they could see up ahead for them, they wouldn't be complaining and whining so much. Every human soul can see what's up ahead for themselves. Someone had mentioned they did not believe in psychic abilities, but they believed that people were intuitive. Psychic or intuitive is the same thing. It does not matter what you call it. You're tuning into your core senses, which are communication receptors with worlds beyond this one. All souls have this ability to read better for themselves than anyone else can. Accurately reading for yourself or anyone is impossible when your ego is ruling the show that is your life.

How often have you received an internal jolt that something in particular was about to happen, and then it did? Even the non-believers can take a step away and recall those incidents where the psychic phenomena did indeed occur for them. You can do this by raising your vibration and tuning into what's outside of physical distractions. Trust the repeated messages you receive. No one can do that for you better than you can. Have patience and faith that what you desire will work out in your favor in the end. Sometimes it's not what you predicted or what you hoped, but you learn to realize that in the end, how it turns out is much better than you had envisioned. There is a reason you're living the particular life you are at this time.

Heavenly guidance sifts into your consciousness almost effortlessly while in a dreamlike meditative state. When you wake up from sleeping at night, it's almost immediately that you have forgotten your dream, even though you awoke from it minutes ago. This is what it's like before you enter an Earthly human life. Before you enter this life, your memory slate is wiped clean except for hints that include your life purpose. This is similar to your memory being wiped clean when you awaken from a profound dream. Only hints of this dream you had while sleeping are left if at all.

You made a contract with your Spirit team before you entered a human life. In this contract are things like the soul mates you would encounter, the things you would endure, your life purpose, when you will pass on and head back home. This is similar to the dream state when you're sleeping. Your memory is fully restored when you cross back over and head home into the next plane.

Some live an entire Earthly life and do not fulfill their contract completely. They may not come to this realization until the final days on their death bed as a human soul. They realize they are indeed going to leave their physical body. The reality and the fear might hit them at that point. They might say, "Why didn't I forgive him or her?" or "Why didn't I allow love in from this person?" These words filter through your consciousness as you transition home to where you came from in the spirit world. Your Spirit team on the other side greets you along with Archangel Jeremiel. They go over your entire Earthly life. This consists of things such as what you did and what you didn't do. What you did to others and what others did to you. What you accomplished or neglected and so forth.

I receive some pretty common psychic related questions. The first common question is about love. Readers write me frustrated about not being in a love relationship. My Spirit team says that the desperate need to have a lover is what blocks one from obtaining a lover. It's the negative feelings associated with that need which includes a fear that it won't happen. This goes back to the saying: "Let go, let God." When you let go of the negative desire and panic to obtain a lover, then the lover shows up. I can attest for me personally that this is true. Every serious love relationship I have been involved in throughout my entire life to date came to me and developed when I wasn't looking for anything. I was in a state of perfect contentment before it happened, and then it happened naturally.

The second common question is surrounding one's career. Others are trying to figure out what type of career they want, or what job they should go after, and in what industry. The response my Spirit team gives me on that is to think about what your passion is beyond making money and then you have your answer. The desire to chase money as ones sole purpose will leave you dejected. I can also attest that the response to this question was accurate for me. I have never gone after a job or career position for the purpose of monetary gain. I went after it because I had a passion and desire for that type of work or position. The money wasn't on my radar. It ended up flowing in naturally and in great abundance more than expected. The increased financial flow for each work position I accepted in my life was the icing on the cake.

Pay attention to your senses when deciphering the incoming Heavenly guidance while on your life's journey. The guidance could even come in the guises of déjà vu moments. Déjà vu moments can be psychic hits of the future or of the past. The past can be a previous life or someone else's past. This can be the case even though the déjà vu moment is playing out as if you're the main character.

The future is what's to come. This also means not necessarily a vision of what's coming for you personally, but it can be someone around you. The way dreams and clairvoyant images come to you are not always direct. It may show you a particular vision, but one that is not necessarily going to play out exactly in the manner it's being displayed. Clairvoyant hits sometimes need to be decoded and interpreted.

The ego desires things now. I'm impatient myself regardless of knowing what's coming up ahead at times. Part of working on spiritual evolvement is learning the nature of patience and tempering the ego. Sometimes another person's guides will communicate with mine. My guides will then interpret what the other person's guides are relaying. They communicate at a fast pace that it overlaps with one another. It's much different in communicating than the way we do here on Earth in the physical body.

Since all souls are born with measuring psychic gifts, this means you can also all train yourself to pay attention to the input you receive. You can train to give tarot or angel card readings for yourself or for others. It takes work to strip away the materialistic life that you have built up within your DNA in this lifetime. With practice and work, you can be just as capable of giving reads for yourself as a professional psychic reader can.

Those who are professional psychic readers or mediums find it difficult to read for themselves, since their judgment is clouded and not objective. This is why many will read with another reader to receive a read from someone who is not emotionally invested in their life. This is also why many psychics do not read for friends as it becomes a conflict of interest. They have emotion invested in their friend and may bend the read to favor the friend. In the end a false read is given and the friend is not helped. Sometimes it causes the ending of a friendship where the friend feels uncomfortable by what their psychic reader friend has relayed to them.

Searching for the right psychic reader can be challenging and much like searching for the right Doctor. Readers read in a variety of ways. Some are angel readers, some are fortune tellers, others channel messages from the other side, and some use objects, while others use nothing, but their own body. There will be a synastry between you and the reader that feels comfortable for you both. No reader should ever tell you what to do.

For example, they should never instruct you to leave a lover unless of course the lover is abusive. The role of an ethical reader is to simply guide you or inform you of what they are seeing about a particular person or situation in question. They should remain completely objective and neutral in your situation. An ethical reader would say something like, "If you stay with this person, the philandering will continue. It is up to you to decide on your next course of action." You have free will choice to decide what's best for you knowing this information.

I've had angel reads, psychic reads, tarot reads, channel reads, and intuitive reads. Those who use no divination tool, those who use boards, rocks or other devices. I love the craft and all points of view. I love the differing ways that others read. You gain different insights and perspectives with a different reader. It's a personal decision when choosing a reader to go with, just as you would in choosing a relationship. One person may love a reader that someone else did not gravitate towards. There is a synastry between reader and readee.

Sometimes others who enjoy the craft love to know what methods other readers use when reading cards. When using a card deck, I do not always use the three card spread. I've rarely if ever used the past-present-future spread or Celtic Cross spread. I don't have a pattern that I stick with when reading. I follow what my Spirit team is telling me through my

Clairaudience channel. I pick the deck up as I'm saying, "I want to know about love for this person." I'm already shuffling before I've finished my sentence. For example, I will hear them say the number six. I nod, "Six. Okay, show me love". Some readers take the top 6 cards off when they're done shuffling. I shuffle for each 6 times until they have me stop on the card. This doesn't mean anyone should do it this way. You adopt the method that works accurately and best for you.

Ask your guides and angels for clarity when you're puzzled by their information. Request they show you signs and symbols to confirm what you're receiving from them. This is one way to determine if you're receiving accurate information or if it's your ego dominating the read. Every soul is born in tune to the other side and connected to God. The more a human soul allows their physical surroundings to influence them, the further away from God and heavenly communication you go.

Do I Volunteer Information to Others?

It is best to avoid volunteering psychic related information to others unless they've asked you for it. It's not particularly enjoyable watching others head for a cliff and not being able to say anything. You cannot interfere with others free will choice. They have to learn lessons on their own. I just keep it to myself unless I'm specifically asked if I'm *seeing* anything. There is the asking me what is the best course of action to take with a decision. I let them know what I'm getting. It goes through one ear out the other. They do the opposite, then come back to me to say, "Okay you were right, now what do I do? How do I get out of this?" It's uncomfortable to not come off as if you're shattering someone's dreams. I'm all for one going after what they want. They're very excited about something and you do not want to crush that for them. You see it being a dead end or not ending well, and they ask you about it. You have to be delicate in the delivery of what you're getting, while still allowing them their free will choice to make the ultimate decision while also being supportive too.

I'm Hearing Voices Telling Me They're Going to Kill Me!

Another common inquiry I receive is someone hearing voices that they are going to kill them. The inquiry comes to me wondering if it's a spirit on the other side. When one is hearing harmful voices, then this is typically the voice of ego. Spirits in Heaven only communicate with love, while the ego communicates in hate and negativity. If it's a demon possession, they would take over your entire soul and body, but those cases are extremely rare despite how common it seems in Hollywood horror films.

The harmful spirits in limbo mode that feed off a human soul's addictions merely prompt that human soul to dive harder into a particular addiction. They don't have the kind of power to whisper they're going to kill that soul. It would defeat their purpose as well, since their goal is simple. It is to get high through the human soul's addiction or vice.

If you're hearing negative voices speaking to you, it's important to first rule out if you've had a traumatic experience in your life. Sometimes traumatic events in one's life trigger negative self talk where it feels as if an entity or spirit is saying harmful negative things to you. Some post traumatic stress side effects cause one's mind to splinter into different selves where it feels as if it's not you saying particular harmful things, but an entity or spirit. It can happen months or even years after the traumatic event. Most people have had at least one traumatic event or circumstance they can recall through the duration of their life that stands out. It can be something seemingly insignificant to someone else, but which is not to you. Circumstances such as a love relationship breakup that left you wounded and depressed.

If the harmful voices are something that continues indefinitely, then it's best to seek out a mental health practitioner to adequately treat and/or diagnose the underlying cause. This can also rule out any deeper issues that might reside within you that need addressing and healing. The next step recommended is to go to a highly evolved healer, counselor, or therapist as you continue down your individual spiritual path.

Questions such as this one can be uncomfortable to answer, but the response is always the same. This type of question is best suited for a mental health professional. It's not my or anyone else's jurisdiction to diagnose a mental health issue, but left for someone medically qualified. It would be poor etiquette and bad practice on my part. I can only offer what my Spirit team relays to me, which is the same response for most common questions. There is nothing wrong with seeking a professional who specializes with mental disorders. One's mental health is extremely vital, and being someone who has fragmented and split off as a child, I understand the importance of addressing it. This is in order to take care of it and examine the underlying cause, so that you can be clear minded. With practice, you will be able to decipher what are your guides and angels, and when your ego mind is playing tricks on you. There is nothing wrong with seeking a professional who specializes with mental disorders. One's mental health is extremely vital, and being someone who has fragmented and split off into various selves as a child, I understand the importance of addressing it. This is in order to take care of it and examine the underlying cause, so that you can be clear minded. With practice, you will be able to decipher what are your guides and angels, and when your ego mind is playing tricks on you.

The "Over Soul" and "Walk-In"

There is what some call an *Over Soul*. Your soul has a higher self and a lower self, and both are distinctively different selves. To some it would appear to be that all human souls have a split personality to an extent. This is depending on how often they vacillate from their higher to their lower self on any given day. Yet it's only one soul, not two. Everyone has a dark side and a light side.

There are cases where a soul will take over another soul's body at some point in their life. It is noticeable to others around them after this happens. The rare soul switching happens during a traumatic event such as a car accident or near death experience. This is where the soul switching takes place. Both souls agreed to have the switching prior to their Earthly life.

Once the soul switching takes place, others begin to notice the individual is not quite the same person they once knew. A pivotal event prompts the person to do a turnaround. They have suddenly changed their views; career, lovers, lifestyle choices and you name it! They almost seem like a stranger to those they are close to. There are elements that are the same since the memory banks of the previous soul have been transferred to the new soul. It's not like the new soul has amnesia. They're able to subconsciously reach into the memory banks of the previous soul's upbringing, but will not recall much. They will feel a detachment to it as if they weren't personally around for it. Some also call this a *Walk-In*.

CHAPTER FOURTEEN

Psychic Timing

$\mathcal{O}$ne of the questions most often asked in a psychic read is, "When?" When will a particular circumstance happen? They want an exact date as to when they will meet that lover, start that new career, or buy that house. This is understandable since you are in a human body and crave immediate material security. This physical comfort could come in the form of the great job, money, or awesome love for example. When these things do not seem to be forthcoming for a prolonged period of time, you might begin to grow permanently solemn, frustrated or disappointed. This state lowers your vibration which could block or delay the event from taking place. This energy certainly does not bring the event to you any more quickly. It is always best to remain optimistic and cheerful as that energy is what attracts in positive circumstances.

No psychic reader can necessarily predict when something is going to happen for someone. Those in

Heaven who are relaying information to the psychic conduit live in a world without devices such as calendars and clocks. Those are manmade designs to give Earth life some resemblance of structure and order. There is no time that exists for Heaven in the way that human souls have made it on Earth. Therefore it's near impossible for spirit guides and angels to give a particular psychic conduit an accurate time to give to their client as to when an event will take place. Time is fluid to those in the spirit world, so when they see a human soul wanting to know when something will take place, they do their best to give an *estimated* time frame. This time frame should be taken with a grain of salt. There are a great many factors that can and will often delay something from happening with any time frame predicted.

There are psychics who nail timing more times than not, but for the most part it's challenging to nail timing. You are gambling with someone's free will choice, which is unpredictable. I've nailed timing in the past and witnessed it happen later. I have had the person I've relayed the information to come back to me a year later. This was in order to say that something I stated a year ago has come true for them. The majority of the time where I've read for others, I avoid giving timing answers, since that is a dangerous risk. It's rare to predict it on the mark because free will enters the equation. When someone asks for timing on something, I will rarely relay it unless I hear a month or date slam into my aura during the read. The circumstances where I offered accurate timing were voluntarily on my part because my Spirit team happened to be highlighting a month, day or season through my clairaudience channel. I just included it as part of the read. If they say nothing as to when something will happen, then I will say, "I don't know. Soon." There are reasons they're not telling the human soul. Sometimes information is on a need to know basis. Your ego wants to know when something is going take place. Your higher self is not interested in the when or how. It knows all is well and what is intended will be.

The timing that is given by a reader is the *probable timing* pending that you or other circumstances connected to your desire are not hindered by any of the party's free will. Free will is not taken seriously enough when it comes to a psychic read. Most human souls operate using free will choice. They rarely listen to their guides and angels. It is more about obtaining their desire immediately. For example, in a love read no one can predict the impulsive choices you or this potential lover might make on any given day. This alters what was originally predicted to happen.

There is a danger when a psychic gives someone a time frame as to when an event will happen. If the time frame the psychic gave comes and goes, then the one who was read for will debunk the psychic as being inaccurate or that it just isn't in the cards for them. Yet, months or even years down the line, it turns out that the event does eventually take place, but it is so far into the future that they've forgot all about the read to begin with.

When I was sixteen years old, my Spirit team had told me that I would be working in the entertainment business in the "near future". I didn't know what the near future was and I didn't ask them when exactly. I just knew without a doubt that it would happen. Of course, I didn't sit around waiting for it to land on my door step. I actively began researching the business at the library and investigating potential companies I could possibly work at.

To make a long story short, years passed and I was still researching and trying to get in. I grew frustrated and disheartened at times, but the desire to get in did not stop me. Weeks after my 23rd birthday, I was offered a position working for a major Hollywood actress at the time. This is to illustrate that I was shown this would happen at sixteen years old and in the near future. The event happened when I turned twenty-three. This dream came to fruition at full throttle about seven years *after* I clairvoyantly saw it coming initially. The point is that it did happen eventually. Can you imagine if I went to a psychic reader who told me, "You'll get into the entertainment business within the coming year?" I might have given up and said, "Oh they were wrong, that never happened." This is why psychic timing cannot always be accurately predicted on the mark. If it is, then keep an open mind that the reader is merely estimating the probable future. Just because the event doesn't take place when they said it would, does not necessarily mean that it won't ever happen.

One way to look at it is that a reader or your own guides and angels are informing you that something is indeed intended to happen. Don't worry yourself over the when and how it will happen. Otherwise you'll drive yourself into a mental obsession. This obsession is what lowers your vibration. When you are in a state of joy and contentment, in the here and now, then this raises your vibration. This then allows positive events to unfold, and even greater opportunities to reach you sooner than later.

I'm one of the most impatient people I know, so this is something I can relate to. I know what it's like to want to know when something is going to take place and how frustrating it can be when time has gone by and nothing has come to pass. Heaven says to trust, have patience, and keep the faith. Know that the path you're on is the way it is for a reason. The choices you've previously made have led you to the place you're currently in. What you desire will reveal itself to you at just the right time. Speaking from personal experience, I can attest that this is true.

Additionally, it's important to remember to follow the nudges, signs, and guidance that you're Spirit team are putting in front of you. If they are constantly dropping the same signs in front of you to go to a different part of town you normally go to, or another store that is off your typical route, then trust that. It could be they are trying to orchestrate something beneficial for you. A psychic reader can rarely assist you with something like this. They might tell you that you're going to meet your next lover in October. October comes and goes and you wonder why it never happened. Were you sitting around at home hiding out between the day of your psychic read and October? This makes it impossible for any lover to find you unless that soul mate rings your doorbell like the postman or delivery person.

When a psychic informs you about a probable situation coming up, then keep an open mind. Take steps that can help it come along to you more readily.

If this is a love partner entering the picture, then this means get outside and mix with other souls. Go out more often so that this wonderful lover can bump into you. Pay attention to your Spirit teams nudges on where to go if you're confused.

While out and about, if this potential lover approaches you and strikes up a friendly conversation, then let your guard down and throw on the charm with them. Smile, be engaging, warm and open. You might not be immediately aware that this person is the potential right away when they approach you. They might not be what you were originally envisioning or thought of, so you end up closing yourself off to someone who desires to engage with you in conversation.

Another important action step can be that it is you who will approach this lover, instead of waiting for them to approach you. This is an easy step for an extroverted soul. If you're an introvert, then practice using your gifts of non-verbal telepathic communication on this potential. You can do this with a smile or by giving them a simple, "Hello." Pay attention to their body language and how responsive or unresponsive they are. This also means pay attention to your own body language. Do you stiffen up to a block of ice with an expressionless face when this person enters your vicinity and notices you?

This is a cold closed off world and some souls may have an automatic fight or flight response. They could be stunned that someone said hello to them let alone an attractive stranger. They might button up and turn away from you or give you a grunt of a response. Does that mean they're not interested? Not necessarily.

When you're in tune to your surroundings, you can gauge whether someone is interested or not. Watch for the subtle cues in their body movement. Do they pull away from you feeling uninterested, angry or threatened? And do they suddenly soften and move back towards you with acknowledgment? Their movements may be subtle that you might not notice it right away. You assume they're not interested, when they may either be shy or thrown off that someone good looking is engaging with them.

Unless someone has been drinking in a bar to loosen up, most people are not used to others being nice to them, especially if you live in an overpopulated big city. Going to a bar or club with the goal of hoping to meet your long term relationship soul mate is a mistake and you'll wind up disappointed. Unless you're someone who loves hanging in a bar and looking for that like minded soul who enjoys the same drinking habits.

If you're a woman, you might have a traditional way of believing how relationships should form. This is where you prefer the guy approaches you and strikes up a conversation. That was the way things once were, but times are significantly different. Now both men and women have to do the work if they want to find a long term loving relationship. If you're a woman, then you approach him with a hello.

If you're interested in a same sex love relationship, then you have additional factors that come into play or ones that might cross your mind. They might be things such as, "What if I approach this person and they don't go my way?" Or what if they have a negative reaction to my sexuality? Of course, you would use precautions regardless of what your sexuality is when approaching a stranger. You're not going to blurt out: "Hey, I'm interested in you!" This method could work, but being subtle and polite in your approach can go a long way. This is where you are striking up a conversation as if it were a potential friend. You'll eventually pick up on enough energy vibrations off the other person to determine what their interest level is. There are human souls who are super sociable and friendly. It doesn't mean they're necessarily seeing you as a potential lover.

Your Spirit team is not going to drop the great lover at your doorstep if you're hiding out at home and you never go out to mingle. They're not going to drop an awesome career opportunity in your life if you've never sent your resume or credentials out to potential employers. Heaven helps those who help themselves. They help those they see are taking action steps to make it happen. When you're passionate and positively driven to achieve this desire, then it's that much quicker to arrive.

CHAPTER FIFTEEN

Grieving, Depression, Suicide

*T*here are souls who have been born into their current Earthly life with emotional or mental challenges. You reside in a cutthroat ego dominating world that has the attitude of *kill or be killed.* This hyper technological age has diminished face to face interaction and trained others to conduct themselves like cold aloof robots. The more sensitive souls struggle to stay afloat while battling a consistent array of depression symptoms in the mix of this. There is a difference between being born into this life with a brain chemistry imbalance to feeling the occasional depression blues. Depression blues that hit you once in a rare while can be triggered by poor lifestyle choices or a negative circumstance that knocks you off cloud nine. Those who experience the rare blues usually bounce back if their innate personality is typically upbeat and optimistic. There are those who have always suffered from depression and anxiety symptoms their entire Earthly life.

How many babies do you know that display depression and anxiety symptoms? There are not very many reported cases. Babies displaying frequent agitating emotions such as crying and screaming could easily be considered to being those human souls who are born more in tune to their environment than others. They're more likely to develop ongoing depression and anxiety symptoms. Yet, it is not that cut and dry. There are babies who are relatively calm and who are just as in tune to their environment with a heightened psychic connection. Perhaps you grew up more sensitive to your environment than someone who operates from a place of oblivion and ego. Depression and anxiety symptoms develop more rapidly in those more sensitive and in tune to their surroundings.

You've likely watched fish swimming in a fish tank. You tap on the glass and the fish abruptly turns skittish and darts in the other direction. This is similar to approaching one with heightened psychic receptors with the other side. Incidentally, the fish behavior is right on target with an evolved soul born in the sign of Pisces. They're floating through life in the dreamy depths of feeling and emotion, but slamming on the gas when a hostile energy enters its vicinity. The other side is the more aggressive image of the Pisces in the form of the shark. The shark is extremely psychic with heightened sensory overload able to pick up on the tiniest molecule of blood floating in the ocean. The shark keeps to itself, but is ready to brutally attack at the slightest provoking. It is not one to get into a cage with. Connect this with those evolved or evolving in the sign of Pisces. Pisces is one of the signs that is extremely sensitive and in tune to what's going on around them. When left unchecked, this can cause regular bouts of depression and anxiety.

Depression and anxiety symptoms that develop and remain within the composites of your soul in this lifetime are not resorted to one having the sign of Pisces somewhere in the top tier of their chart of course. This is merely illustrated to understand the connection to a sensitive soul and how they might react when threatened or provoked. Your sensitivities are a genuine gift from above to use for positive benefits. Many with heightened sensitivity and stimuli turn it into a successful career in the creative world. They are artists, actors, entertainers, painters, writers, photographers and the list goes on and on. When they channel their sensitivities appropriately, there is no telling what they can accomplish. Unfortunately, the down side is when they're unable to channel it positively. Or they vacillate back and forth from channeling it positively and producing striking work to falling into the darkness of depression symptoms. Some depression symptoms are terribly severe that it leads that human soul to commit suicide.

Actor Robin Williams committed suicide on August 11, 2014. This devastated the world. It prompted a discussion in many circles to take depression and suicide seriously. There were the critics popping in that are lucky enough to be cruising through life as happy campers. They made statements such as suicide being a selfish act or that if you're depressed to get over it. These souls are removed from the imbalances created in more sensitive beings due to the harshness of the Earth's environment.

Robin Williams had a super large heart and was a bundle of love joy with an infectious energy. He left the world a legacy and catalog of wonderful movies behind that showcase his brilliant talent. It's a shame he gave up before his time here was complete. He was young with immense possibilities ahead of him. I'm often asked how is it that a person's guides and angels do not stop something like suicide from happening. This is asked as if Heaven isn't doing anything on their end to stop it. They're merely sitting around twiddling their thumbs. Human souls have free will choice in order to learn and grow. No heavenly being can intervene without permission.

Where suicide is concerned, the soul's guide and angel are doing what they can to ease that soul's heart and convince them not to do something that will prove fatal. However, as many sensitive beings understand, when you're experiencing negative emotions such as depression, anger, fear or upset, then you're not picking up on anything outside of yourself, let alone your own Spirit team's communications from Heaven. You're only hearing the shouting negativity of your own thoughts which spreads in your mind like a Cancer. It isn't uncommon for comedians to suffer from depression, let alone entertainers and especially gifted actors. They are highly tuned in psychic sensitive sponges able to walk in someone else's shoes. They hold the least amount of judgment by being able to look at a cruel person and find that person's heart when playing a character. Having grown up and worked in the entertainment business, I see them as just like everybody else. They have immense success and talent, but they are struggling with internal issues just like much of the world.

Depression, anxiety and highly sensitive people are not reserved to comedians and entertainers. A great deal of human souls born into this lifetime and those beyond are ultra sensitive. They've been planted on Earth or we should say plopped in the middle of a battlefield. Hostile and barbaric human souls surround the sensitives in this world. They tamper and wreak harsh energy that causes long term side effects on the more evolved and evolving souls.

Someone who was bullied growing up by other kids will choose to turn the dark into something light. They'll make light of the darkness by making jokes about it and everything else. For some this might not be enough if the internal turmoil goes untreated. You then resort to drugs and alcohol to quiet the demons and to feel happy if just for five minutes. The physical life at times becomes too overbearing on souls battling with ongoing depression. As for Robin Williams, they say he was growing older and his previous marriages were costing him a fortune long after they were over. The great movie projects to work on were coming in less and less. Some speculated this led him to end his life. Many souls have experienced career set backs or relationships that drained you emotionally or financially, but they don't end their life. There are other chemical imbalances at play that push one to come to the conclusion that a suicide will be carried out.

Your life rarely stays the same. Circumstances are always changing. Although it can be tough navigating through life changes, you do not have to do it alone.

Call on your heavenly team of guides and angels who are on standby to make these changes more manageable. Be open to knowing that change is good. Maybe you'll need to downsize or budget more efficiently. A simplified life is all human souls really need. When you leave this Earthly life, you're not taking anything with you. You're not taking your clothes or toothbrush.

Some commit suicide due to perpetual feelings of abandonment and loss. For others it is a conflict between their higher and lower selves to the point where the higher self is left perpetually in the dark. None of what is experienced is real, but in the mind contemplating suicide, it is making it real and giving it quite a bit of unstoppable attention. The Full Moon heightens depression symptoms, making the feelings more exacerbated. Incidentally, Robin Williams took his life during the peak of the Full Moon energy. Within a day after he passed on, his soul was doing fine and fell into the lower 5% of souls who take their lives and cross over without any issues. It's important to take depression seriously and get the treatment necessary to continue on. It's also important to remember the body of work that one has donated for the improvement of humanity. This is what will remain alive in years to come, rather than the matter of how ones soul moved into the next plane.

A puzzled reader asked, "Why is taking your life bad?"

There are many violent ways in which a soul's life might end in its lifetime. There is a stigma that taking one's life is bad. It's not bad for anyone, but that particular soul. Many offer varying theories as to why it's bad, but I can only say what I've been shown by my own Spirit team.

When someone takes their own life via free will, they do so before their time. When this happens, their soul goes into a state of shock as it crosses over. The state that you're in as you cross over stays relatively the same. If you had a large ego, that large ego is still intact as you're crossing over. If you were suffering from depression and you took your own life, that state you were in when you took your own life is still present as your soul is crossing over. It's not a pleasant way to cross over because you took your life for the hope of release, but you're still not released long after your soul has been extricated from your temporary body. Luckily, there is a process that takes place in restoring that soul to full capacity. There's a delay before that happens. Sometimes the soul who took their life is disoriented. It is also important to note that there is no pain when crossing over. Any pain that exists is only when in the physical human body.

There are other things that the soul agreed upon as well when they entered this life. If they take their life prematurely, they end up having to incarnate into another human body and go through similar issues and circumstances all over again. Therefore, it's only bad from the perspective of that soul. It's not bad in the way others preach how you're not supposed to take your own life or you go to Hell. Fortunately that doesn't exist. The real Hell is the life the soul is suffering through. Hell is on Earth. It is one that the ego in corrupt human souls creates. Luckily, that is the worst of the Hell that exists for most.

The contributions Robin Williams made towards humanity on a global scale and throughout the duration of his life were so great that it gave him an edge over a soul who might not have contributed much if anything. The contributions were beyond just his film work with its positive messages, but it extended into the countless giving and charity works he did outside of that. Included was his overall nature in bringing joy and laughter to so many people. These are major factors that are considered. These factors are what made his soul strong enough to overcome being stuck in suicide mode long after he passed. The positive contributions you give towards humanity never go unnoticed in Heaven even if no one notices on Earth. It is indeed recorded on the other side.

He was worked with in Heaven with guides and angels in order to restore his soul. He was out of commission and unreachable the first day he passed on. I was unable to get a connection which gave me a slight concern. The day after his Earthly death, he was present stating he was surrounded by some *very large angels*. These are Archangels he was referring to. He also sounded as if he had awakened from a deep hyper sleep which is often the case with suicides or those souls who face an unexpected and abrupt death such as suicide or at the destructive hands of someone else's free will. Yet, he had cheeriness in his voice that was comforting and let me know he was doing great. Even though he expressed some guilt remains within him surrounding various issues he was faced with as a human soul. He reached a place of forgiveness and his soul was restored in the process.

Often times when a human soul is grieving over the passing of a departed loved one, it pulls the departed soul back into the Earth plane. When you make peace with the one that has passed on, then you release the grieving attachment to them that might keep the soul stuck in this plane. See the soul as exiting through an etheric doorway of heavenly light where they will be doing fantastic! You will see your departed loved one again when your time in this lifetime is complete. In the meantime, they will be with you, watching you, and working with you as one of your guides from time to time. They will be there to greet you when you enter that doorway of light yourself.

Human life is accustomed to losses that cause a heavy dark cloud over ones heart. Losses include the human death of someone close to you or the loss of a deep love relationship that ended. Any loss that causes prolonged grief is included. From the perspective of spirit, there is no real loss in this scenario. These losses are part of the human soul experience, but this is an illusion. They do not exist in the bigger reality of why you are here. Everything you have ever loved or missed comes back to you when your Earthly class is complete. Those grieving over the human death of a loved one must understand that it is not a death in the way that you know it. That soul simply graduated from their Earthly class life run. The uncomfortable heavy weight of the human vessel they occupied was shed. They soared effortlessly into the next room where you will one day re-unite with them. The transition for most is incredibly smooth! There is no pain since pain exists in the Earth's atmosphere. This Earthly life school is equated to boot camp for the soul!

The feeling of grief where you have lost someone you deeply cherished and loved can be challenging to overcome. It is really fear of the unknown, or not seeing concrete proof that their loved one is still around. The ego mind, which is detached from spirit, conjures up all sorts of conclusions of the worst possible scenarios that there is no next life. As a human soul, it is a process of adjustment when the one you love is not in front of you. Yet it doesn't mean that they're gone in the real reality sense. You will be seeing your loved ones again when your Earthly run is complete. All that you loved and lost will be present when your class here is over. As your grieving dissolves, you grow more in tune to your surroundings. Grief blocks heavenly communication and you're unable to notice when the loved one is communicating with you from the other side. Over time as you raise your vibration from grief, you'll notice the signs and ways your departed loved one is saying 'hello' or communicating with you in the interim.

If you battle with emotional and mental issues in this lifetime such as depression and anxiety, know that you are more psychically in tune than you realize. There is assistance out there in finding healthful ways to temper it or control the onslaught of depression emotions experienced.

CHAPTER SIXTEEN

Find the Love Within

It's easy to lose sight of why you're here. The way human life has been set up and structured by the ego in others has caused enormous discontent. Human ego trained other souls to be unhappy and glum by thriving for nonsense. Not everyone is affected by the harsh energies of the planet. These people have made adjustments to their lifestyle choices. This includes living in areas of nature with little to no chaos and people. Watching what they ingest in their physical bodies and taking care of it through daily exercise. They ensure the people they surround themselves with are high vibrational. They avoid the negativities of social media, the internet and gossip entertainment.

There are a great many positives to Earthly life. Human souls took what they innately learned from the spirit world and built homes, created work and jobs for others, designed transportation, as well as an ease of communication through advanced technological devices. This is some of the fantastic concrete necessities for human life. These are practical ways of surviving on a planet that is spilling over the edges. However, interpersonal relationships continue to suffer sliding rapidly on a decline. Love is lacking, while cruelty and unfriendliness is gaining. It is true that human souls manage to find the love when a crises hits. They intervene when they notice someone is being pushed down, but the love they exude in those instances is temporary. You grow lost in the nonsense of the noise of the ego. Some are consumed by jobs they're not happy in, or you're living check-to-check, or struggling to find work. Perhaps you're in relationships that are unsatisfying, or you're perpetually single longing for a long-term committed love relationship that never surfaces. You're forced to be in situations you do not want to be in. What an effort it is to get to a place of feeling eternally happy.

When you're faced with circumstances that do not jive with your higher self, examine how you arrived at that place. Look at the underlying cause that has prompted you to feel negative when this happens. Identify it, and then dig deep into understanding why it has upset you. There are circumstances that no doubt have made you angry or prompted feelings of discomfort. Maybe you ran into someone at the store who was rude to you. You being a sensitive absorbed that like nobody's business. It ends up putting you in a funk. For some sensitive's, they'll be angry for a minute, others for hours, or you could be one of those who immerses in the energy for the rest of the day. Avoid beating yourself up over it. It just means that you're a hyper sensitive psychic sponge. You have compassion and love within you as all souls do, even though this might be difficult to grasp. Whenever you witness ugliness in someone else, remember that they were born with the deepest love and compassion beyond measure. What you're observing with them is the darkness of ego at its best. This soul has given its power away to their lower self and ego. The ego cannot be reasoned with or convinced of anything, but of what it wants. The ego seeks to sabotage themselves or others. It can be someone who slanders a product they did not care for. A high vibrational soul who is not pleased with something does not waste its time resorting to negativity or in giving it any attention. It only focuses on the products it enjoyed.

When you witness aggression or disrespectful behavior flying at you, then you will absorb that energy. It seeps into your aura and soul. It causes an array of negative circumstances and moods to assault you. What is important is that you find positive exercises that can assist you in releasing it and letting that go. It might feel easier said than done, but when a slight happens in your world, your ego has trouble letting go of it. When you understand this concept of separating yourself from the troublesome ego, it becomes simpler to manage and temper it.

When you have a higher degree of sensitivity than other souls, then you are more likely to be affected by someone else's ego. You're a psychic sponge who easily absorbs the negative or off putting energies in others. It is a gift, but at times it can feel like a curse when you enter environments with human souls displaying low vibrational behavioral patterns. You absorb that negative energy which drops your mood affecting your inner and outer world.

When you grow negative, moody, or agitated, then this is a sign of two possible conclusions. One is that you've ingested low vibrational foods or drinks. Or you may have absorbed this energy from someone toxic you crossed paths with.

It can even be a stranger on the sidewalk who walked passed you. If they're displaying low vibrational behavior, then that energy is lodged in their aura. As a tuned in sensitive psychic sponge, you've absorbed that into your aura sometimes without knowing it. Although, the super tuned in psychic sponges are typically aware they just absorbed this energy from someone in passing.

The souls you absorbed this energy from do not always intend to have a low vibration. It's usually done innocently and naively, or sometimes in other words, not knowing any better. Some souls have not evolved enough to be more in tune to something outside of themselves. This is partially why that particular soul is living an Earthly life.

Those in tune with the other side, the soul and spirit, are turned off by harsh people and energies. They steer clear of those who perpetually display low vibrational traits. This can be from the guy trying to pull a fast one by nickel and diming someone to buy a car. We call them pushy salespeople. They do not care about you. They only care about what's in your wallet. They have a quota and if they want to keep that particular job, they know they need to do whatever it takes to sell a car! There are easy going salespeople who do indeed care about you and do not display shark attack like behavior. They do not attempt to find ways to sell you something when you're having doubts or feeling uncomfortable about it. This type of salesperson will simply say, "I'm here to answer any questions you have about any of this. If you're interested, then let me know."

It can be your employer or someone you work with who puts on the fakeness whenever you enter the room. As a tuned in soul, you can smell them a mile away. They're threatened by your higher frequency energy. They subconsciously know that you're on to them. This also turns off a lower vibrational energy in someone else. Low vibrational human souls are threatened by someone who exudes a high vibrational energy. The low vibrational soul's ego feels out of your league. High vibrational people don't feel threatened by others unless that person is exuding negative energy traits. They're not threatened, but are rather repulsed.

It's not always this cut and dry. Sometimes it can also be that you and these other people you come into contact with don't know each other well enough to accept your differences.

There was an incident in my former days where I was working for an employer who rubbed everyone the wrong way. I have never in the history of my soul's life ever warranted that behavior any attention, but I noticed others coming to me here and there to express how this woman upsets them. There was one day when someone pointed out to me something negative about her.

I responded, "Yeah, I'm hearing that quite a bit. It's best to ignore it."

They said, "I guess that's all one can do."

That banter got me thinking about this woman. I decided to make a pact to meet her half way. I would throw on the charm and friendliness. The next day I went into her office unannounced and sat in her guest chair. She was all business asking if there was something I needed.

I said, "No, I'm just visiting. Wanted to say hi and see how you're doing."

She seemed a little stunned as if no one had bothered to do that before. Although the business armor and cold reserve was still up, I noticed she flinched and softened slightly allowing just a little bit of light out. She attempted to engage with me and make some small talk. For me personally, this was an effort, since I dislike small talk and I rarely approach others unless necessary. Something miraculous soon happened where we started this lighthearted dialogue banter.

The next day I went back to see her at some point to see how she was doing again. I proceeded to do that every day realizing we were bonding and hitting it off. Soon it was no longer an effort for me to chill with her briefly or for her to engage. Both of our reserves were coming down. Once I tore down those walls and met her half way, not only did the morale within the production company improve, but our connection improved as well. We were not just two cold ice conquerors going toe to toe. In those days, I was much darker and colder than I am now. She started to open up a little bit more as time went by. To make a long story short, at the time of this writing, I've known her personally for over 18 years now! She's a wonderful soul with an amazing generous heart. Yet, when others have asked how I met her, I go back into time and remember that it didn't start off that way. Sometimes when you take the time to know someone who has the cold reserve up, you discover they're not as hostile as they are coming off.

This coldness and reserve has grown in others thanks to the technological age. Newer and future generations are being raised on devices that train you to be lacking in honest face-to-face soul connections. For those that have gone out on a date, you've probably noticed some of the typical preliminary questions. They want to know what your job is or what kind of work do you do. What kind of car do you drive? These ego driven questions are externally based. Your job does not define you in real reality, but the human ego has set their life up in a way that their whole world revolves around what kind of job you do. Who cares what you do for a living. Unless you're working in a field that is your passion and it brings you joy, then it is irrelevant what kind of work you do. This passion is your life purpose, but many do not work in jobs that are their passion. For most, it is a paycheck that squeezes the life force out of that soul. They're usually under stress and grumbling about life in general.

When you absorb the ions of negative and cold energy around you, then this can put a damper on your spirit until you address it. You can sit around and hope that something amazing will happen around you that will suddenly raise your vibration, or you can address it and do something about it immediatelIt can be going for a walk in a nature setting. This is followed by taking deep healthy breathes in and requesting that your spirit team release any and all negative energy that has latched onto your soul. It can be getting together with an optimistic friend who observes healthy life choices, or someone who always lifts your aura just by being in your vicinity. You can throw on a funny movie or make love to your relationship partner. What you're trying to do is re-raise your vibration. Taking basic soul enhancing steps when an assault has attacked your aura can do the trick.

A Vibration Raising Exercise

Everyone has experienced some hard times at one time or another. You have negative things to say about it. The ego fixates on the horrid that came out of that. Rise above your ego and ask yourself, "What greatness did I get out of that experience? What was awesome about it?"

The soul's experiences happen for a reason regardless if they're challenging or not. It is not because you did something to deserve it, but because your soul is destined for greatness. You're here in this Earthly life school to find ways that suit you in order to enhance your soul and spirit. You're not here to find out the latest sale on jeans or rip through relationships selfishly with no care in the world. In order to improve, you have much to gain. When something negative happens in your world, work on looking at it from an optimistic perspective.

An exercise you can do is to pick up a journal or a notebook. Use that notepad as your diary to put in only optimistic viewpoints in your life. When you find that you're buried heavily in negative thoughts and emotions unable to break away, take a moment to pull the notebook out. Devote a page or more to whatever it is that is upsetting you. If it's a person, then write that person's name in your journal entry. Instead of focusing on what they did to upset you or whatever circumstance has upset you, shift that into something positive. Think about all of the qualities you love about the person that has angered you. Remove your ego from the equation and look at that person through the eyes of an egoless angel. List everything that is positive about them and how that affects you in an optimistic way. I know some may grumble when reading that, and believe me I understand. I have an ego too! When someone has hurt or angered you, of course it's going to be difficult to see them through the eyes of love. Know that when you're looking at them through the eyes of love, you're not condoning their behavior and nor do you have to remain best friends with them. You're doing this exercise as a release. It's for your benefit in order to remove that old, tired, angry energy you're carrying around that surrounds the person or circumstance. You do not need that energy, but in order to release it, acknowledging it with love is what raises your vibration. When your vibration is raised you are more apt to receiving clearer communication from the spirit world, which in turn assists you on your path towards abundance in all forms.

Your mind may begin to wander to all of the things you feel this person has done that has hurt or upset you. However, you will not write those things down. Remember this is a positive journal. You will immediately adjust your thoughts back to the positive things about this person. Let's say it was an ex-lover who cheated on you, was abusive, or left you and the relationship. You will not write any of those things down, but rather will focus on their good qualities. If you're only able to come up with one good quality, then write that one down. It is an exercise that takes much effort in this case, because you're holding anger towards this person for doing one or all of the things I suggested. Your ego refuses to see the goodness in someone who has upset or hurt you.

If it is a circumstance that happened to cause you upset, then you will write down in this journal the optimistic features that have come out of that. For example, you receive a traffic ticket. Instead of focusing heavily on how you have no time to take care of the ticket, or no money to pay for it, write down the positive benefits that you've gained from the ticket. You might write something down like: "This has taught me to drive more carefully." That statement feels far better than saying, "I have no money. How am I going to pay for this! It wasn't even my fault!"

This exercise may not immediately change your life, but it will gradually guide you into positively changing your life. It will assist you in getting into the habit of bouncing back from upsetting situations much more quickly. It will help you to view circumstances and people in a more positive light. The key is if you're going to play this game, then you have to play objectively. Putting all things positive and optimistic in this journal is the exercise. Only write your blessings, appreciations and gratitude for situations and people in your life. This absolutely includes everything and everyone that causes you to feel negative emotions. This might be challenging, but in the end it will be rewarding as you are re-training your mind to think positively. This raises your vibration in the process, which assists with attracting in positive circumstances and people to you over the course of time. Because it raises your vibration, it also clears out the debris that accumulates in and around the communication line to Heaven and your Spirit team. If it doesn't do anything, but allow you to start shining your true loving light, then that is all that matters in the end.

The ego is a wretched problem seeker. It might appear to be louder than your higher self and your Spirit team of guides and angels. This is due to a couple of factors. The atmosphere of the Earth plane is extremely thick and dense that connecting to the other side through all of the toxic debris makes it challenging. Your guides and angels are louder and more powerful than any ego. Yet, when the soul is in the Earth dimension, the communication lines are heavier and dirtier. The ego rises through the dirt. It already rises as soon as your soul enters into this human life. The ego is activated in a big way. When the soul is in the earth plane it's like roaming through life with ear plugs on. Anyone who has put ear plugs on to sleep at night may point out how they can sometimes faintly hear light sounds with them on. The higher self strains to hear Heaven through this muffled sound. When a human soul lives in a higher vibrational state, this allows light in, which gives rise to the higher self. Suddenly that soul is hearing their guides and angels more clearly than usual.

You are not alone as you are surrounded by at least one Spirit Guide and one Guardian Angel from your human birth until human death. They assist you down the right path in order to fulfill your purpose while here. When you are in your higher self's state you connect with your Spirit team on the other side with greater efficiency. When you are in your lower self's state or ego, then you block heavenly guidance and messages that keep you on the right path and assist you in achieving your desires. In my connections with Heaven, I've discovered that all are loved and seen through the eyes of love. Do your best to keep the darkness of your ego in check and exude love full time!

CHAPTER SEVENTEEN

Wise One, Hunter, Indigo

Personal Story – The Afterword

$\mathscr{I}$ am described as an Indigo in some circles. These are the souls that are the dark, intense, fighters of the light. Many of them were born in the 1970's and into the early 1980's. I'm also a Wise One therefore it is a double whammy of strength and hardheaded force. Sometimes it's too much intensity that I cannot always control, because half the time I'm unaware of it until it comes out. It's been a part of my DNA and my consciousness for as long as I can remember. It's like trying to reign in a horse stampede. I'm compassionate to a degree, but there's a lot of fiery warrior strength within that compassion. There are days where it's too much even for me, so I know it can be too much for others. To always be on guard and have the invisible armor up ready to go to battle every second can be exhausting. I'm making it sound like I don't relax. I relax and take it easy quite a bit when I can. Daily exercise and centering myself in nature and watching what I put into my body. In fact, others have used the phrase *'calm inside the storm'* when describing me. There's that visible calm strength when others around me are consumed by chaos. However, inside the wheels are always turning.

You pray for those who are absorbed in drama and chaos, or you enlighten them with words that will knock the wind out of their sails. The messages and guidance fall into me from above and it suddenly gets quiet around me. Someone says something that I know is not of truth and my eyes narrow. I'm thinking, "This person doesn't know that you cannot lie to me or try to pull a fast one. You will not get very far." They suddenly get uncomfortable because I don't hide that I know. Even if I don't verbally say anything, I've been told that it's written all over my face.

My fight has always been aimed at improving humanity, even if it means playing bad cop. And I don't like to play bad cop, but if it's for the greater good, then it comes naturally. It's not in me to remain silent otherwise they would've had someone else do the job. I'm as hard on myself as I am on others if not more. Ultimately, my fight along with Heaven is intended to get others to wake up to love. Love and respect others and this planet and yourself. That's really all it is. The fight is all about love in the end. It's the reason we exist. It's the reason we're here. It's bringing the love out. It's getting everybody to pay more attention to how they treat others and how they treat themselves. It's raising their consciousness one person at a time so this world and everyone in it can finally feel a sense of peace and joy. This sounds incredibly simple, but it's severely lacking. Do you notice this love and respect energy in everyone you come into contact with?

Human souls have a tendency to operate from their lower selves and ego unable to control it in when it happens. They live in that space 24/7. This is tiring on your soul and body to live that way. Those who partake in vibration raising methods or who are connected to their soul have an ego, but they wrestle with it less than someone who is disconnected full time. I'm in a human body in this dense compressed atmosphere. I most certainly wrestle with my lower self and ego from time to time. It was far worse growing up as I allowed the human tampering of my upbringing to dictate how it was supposed to be. Even though I knew it was wrong according to God's law. Catch yourself when you fall into the space of ego and lower self, then work on raising your vibration again. For the most part, I do my best with what I'm given and to remain centered and connected.

I have some elements and qualities of what others describe as a Knight Paladin incarnate. This is due to the Knights having half the Wise One traits where I hail from in the spirit world. They are my soul brothers and sisters on the other side. We reside and mix and mingle in the same circles. The actual Knights Paladin are a bit taller than me and more compassionate. They are the strong silent types you witness in some of the soldiers in the military. They're also extremely loyal and committed to their work and their love relationships. I've incarnated into this body that is 5' 7½". Those that incarnate from the Knights realm tend to be taller, but not always. I *see* the hybrids that have some of the Wise One nature as being part of the same Wise One tribe. They move in and out of the Wise One realm in the spirit world. There are Wise One Knights, Wise One Angels, and Wise One Stars, to name a few among some of the others in the spirit world. They all take various forms, but it's all connected to the realm of the Wise One. As a full blooded Wise One, I know the ego all too well.

The tribe of the Wise Ones I hail from are hunters. I have a book devoted to all things Wise One appropriately titled, *Realm of the Wise One*. Wise Ones are the fighters, soldiers and hunters from the other side in the literal sense. Some wear the knight armor, others wear the cloak, and some carry the bow and arrow. The hunters move at the speed of light back home as most do. They jump and move very quickly, so many of them who incarnate into an Earthly life tend to be a little shorter than the Knights. They're big on exercise, always physically active and on the go, pending of course that they weren't born into this life with physical challenges.

Falling into my ego and lower self once caused a manifested physical accident. Depression hit me out of nowhere due to a former love relationship break up rising up within me. For years, I had been under much discipline and centered control. Even though I was experiencing uncontrollable feelings of detachment from spirit and a rise in ego coaxing me to feel disconnected and solemn, this did not stop me from physical activity. I went on an exercise excursion that lasted for three hours. Half of that was on a jog and hike on an uphill incline to the top of a mountain with magnificent views. When I arrived back at my destination I felt alive, but this was counteracted with an eerie sadness taking over me. I was losing my serenity. I knew I had to climb back out of the abyss as quickly as possible or there would be repercussions. This decline had not been experienced in my life in years. I was stunned that I was unable to pull out of it as usually I bounce back immediately.

Hours later my left leg developed a slight sprain from this long physical excursion coupled with traces of depression enveloping me. It grew worse as the hours turned into night. The next day back on my home turf, my left leg was not any better. It needed a few more days to get back to optimum levels. I ignored that guidance and went out again for more physical activity.

I thought, "I'll just take it super easy on my activity run."

My body and my Spirit team were sending me a big message not to go out again. It is time for rest.

A friend asked me if I was going back out. I said, "I'm not sure. My left leg is a little sprained from yesterday." I ignored that and thirty minutes later went back out.

I do a lot of obstacle course work on rough terrain when exercising at times. This time as I hopped from one rock to another and then jumped down, I landed incredibly wrong. Crunch. Bam. The pain was out of this world. I don't even know how I made it back home, but I asked for heavenly assistance immediately and I made it home.

On the day of the accident, I wasn't sure what went wrong or if something was broken. I moved into a dark confusion state. Didn't know if I needed to go to the emergency room or not. My Doctor had x-rays taken and it was immediately diagnosed within a couple days. I suffered a high ankle sprain, foot sprain, and a torn tendon and ligament from the calf to the ankle on my left foot. Luckily, nothing was broken. However, I would not be recovered immediately. It would take anywhere from two to six weeks. I used crutches for the first couple of weeks. Wore a beach flip flop on my left foot for four weeks, then I was able to transfer that to a *comfortable* shoe. Worked with a physical therapist after the fourth week to ensure I was healing efficiently.

Many who knew me expressed concern that this happened and added: "This is horrible, because you're so active!"

I'd smile cheery, "Ah, it is what it is. I'll be fine."

Inside it was torture not being able to physically move around much if at all. Moving would require pain and I needed to heal. This was my third work out accident within five years so you would think I would learn. Exercise and being active is like oxygen to me. Others close to me suggested using that time to stop and smell the roses so to speak. I know who I am from the spirit world. I also understand how some of those traits are still within me in this human body. Wise One hunters are always on the go, but there are limitations while in the Earthly human body. You can get injured easily! It's in my nature to explore, hike, jump, jog, bike, move and be active. The hunters in the Wise One realm care about their human body. When it's in your DNA to be on the go, it's difficult to stop. This isn't to say that they never relax, but merely illustrating the challenges they experience when they're suddenly prompted not to move.

Did you note the connection between the depression hit and the aftermath of that? The vibration of the thoughts you have will set in motion what kind of energy vibration will be returned back to you. I fell into a rare temporary slump that doesn't usually happen for me anymore. Regardless, I'm in a human body at this time with a larger than life ego that I do my best to keep under control. I have human love relationship experiences that have ended abruptly without any notable complex issues that would cause one to leave a love relationship. It can be as simple as the one you were involved with received their personal moment of clarity that they are not meant for relationship life. Their soul's path is choosing to go in another direction. As a love addict and someone governed by love, I am most affected by love in this lifetime, especially when it's lacking. I come from a place where a lack of love is considered abnormal, and yet in this physical Earthly life, it has been taught to be the norm. It is the norm due to the darkness of ego in humankind. It's caused negative repercussions and effects on the planet that continue to spiral human life into stress and unhappiness.

I experienced this hit of depression, which manifested itself into my physical body. Granted one could easily point out that I made an error in judgment and that's what caused the workout accident. The ego is complicated, deceptive and it changes form. It causes negative feelings and emotions to rise. When you're experiencing any kind of negative emotion, you may be able to likely pinpoint what transpired from that thought and feeling. If it causes something detrimental to take place, then the flip side is that it can be a blessing in disguise. It wakes you up to notice that you've been out of sorts lately and it's time to re-center. It's time to get happy and let the things go that cannot be controlled. Circumstances happen in your life for a reason. Sometimes it will cause you to feel depressed, angry or even fearful. Note when this rises within you, that you do your best to temper the overwhelming feelings. Avoid doing things that you know you're not ready for no matter how much of a warrior you are!

Let this be the beginning of a new and more improved version of you. Experience the astonishing outpouring of energy and optimism of what is to come. Everything before this moment are the lessons learned that have led you to today. Allow all of the garbage and nonsense of the past burn in a metaphysical bonfire. I've spent my entire life knowing what I wanted and going after it. This mantra continues today as I am always evolving with new goals and interests. If there was a particular job I wanted, I went after it and got it. I wanted to work in the film business with some of the industry's respected talent, I went after that and did that. I wanted to write books and I do that. Avoid allowing your lower self to talk you out of going after what you want as long as it's aligned with your higher self's purpose. Ignore the negative voice that stops you from obtaining your dreams. Allow your higher self to take back the control from your ego. Find the path that leads you to true permanent serenity. This serenity state was the one you were in when you were initially born into an Earthly life.

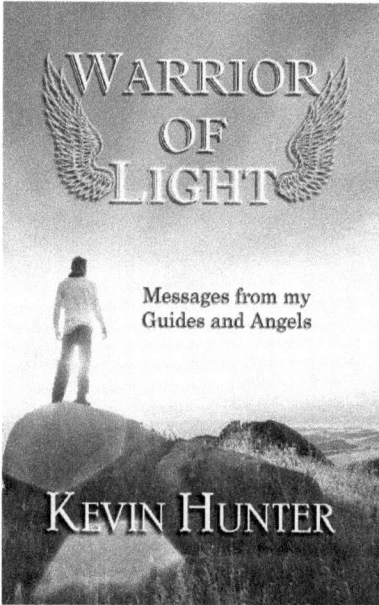

157

The follow up book to *"Warrior of Light: Messages from my Guides and Angels"*, is available in paperback and kindle, by Kevin Hunter

"EMPOWERING SPIRIT WISDOM
A Warrior of Light's Guide on Love, Career and the Spirit World"

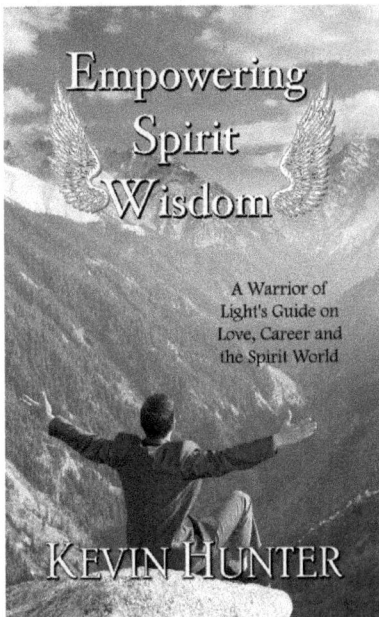

Empowering Spirit Wisdom

A Warrior of Light's Guide on Love, Career and the Spirit World

KEVIN HUNTER

Kevin Hunter relays heavenly, guided messages for everyday life concerns with his book, *Empowering Spirit Wisdom.* Some of the topics covered are your soul, spirit and the power of the light, laws of attraction, finding meaningful work, transforming your professional and personal life, navigating through the various stages of dating and love relationships, as well as other practical affirmations and messages from the Archangels. Kevin Hunter passes on the sensible wisdom given to him by his own Spirit team in this inspirational book. *Empowering Spirit Wisdom* is part two of the Warrior of Light series of books. Part one is called, *Warrior of Light: Messages from my Guides and Angels.*

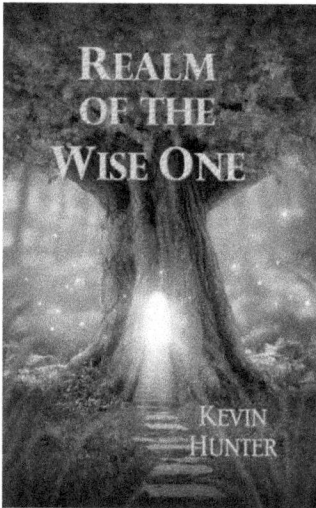

Also available in paperback and kindle by

Kevin Hunter,

"REALM OF THE WISE ONE"

In the Spirit Worlds and the dimensions that exist, reside numerous kingdoms that house a plethora of Spirits that inhabit various forms. One of these tribes is called the Wise Ones, a darker breed in the spirit realm who often chooses to incarnate into a human body one lifetime after another for important purposes. The *Realm of the Wise One* takes you on a magical journey to the spirit world where the Wise Ones dwell. This is followed with in-depth and detailed information on how to recognize a human soul who has incarnated from the Wise One Realm.

Author, Kevin Hunter, is a Wise One who uses the knowledge passed onto him by his Spirit team of Guides and Angels to relay the wisdom surrounding all things Wise One. He discusses the traits, purposes, gifts, roles, and personalities among other things that make up someone who is a Wise One.

Wise Ones have come in the guises of teachers, shaman, leaders, hunters, mediums, entertainers and others. *Realm of the Wise One* is an informational guide devoted to the tribe of the Wise Ones, both in human form and on the other side.

Also available in paperback and kindle by
Kevin Hunter,

"REACHING FOR THE WARRIOR WITHIN"

Reaching for the Warrior Within is the author's personal story recounting a volatile childhood. This led him to a path of addictions, anxiety and overindulgence in alcohol, drugs, cigarettes and destructive relationships. As a survival mechanism, he split into many different "selves". He credits turning his life around, not by therapy, but by simultaneously paying attention to the messages he has been receiving from his Spirit team in Heaven since birth.

Kevin Hunter gains strength, healing and direction with the help of his own team of guides and angels. Living vicariously through this inspiring story will enable you to distinguish when you have been assisted on your own life path. *Reaching for the Warrior Within* attests that anyone can change if they pay attention to their own inner guidance system and take action. This can be from being a victim of child abuse, or a drug and alcohol user, to going after the jobs and relationships you want. This powerful story is for those seeking motivation to change, alter and empower their life one day at a time.

The *Warrior of Light* series of mini-pocket books are available in paperback and E-book by Kevin Hunter called, *Spirit Guides and Angels, Soul Mates and Twin Flames, Divine Messages for Humanity, Raising Your Vibration, Connecting with the Archangels*

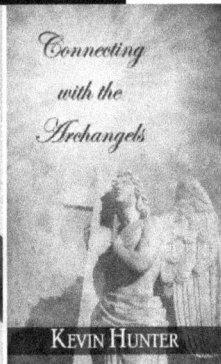

Also available in paperback and E-book by Kevin Hunter, *Ignite Your Inner Life Force*, *Awaken Your Creative Spirit* and *The Seven Deadly Sins*

About Kevin Hunter

Kevin Hunter is an author, love expert and channeler. His books tackle a variety of genres and tend to have a strong male protagonist. The messages and themes he weaves in his work surround Spirit's own communications of love and respect which he channels and infuses into his writing and stories.

His books include the Warrior of Light series of books, *Warrior of Light: Messages from my Guides and Angels, Empowering Spirit Wisdom, Realm of the Wise One, Reaching for the Warrior Within, Darkness of Ego, Ignite Your Inner Life Force, Awaken Your Creative Spirit,* and *The Seven Deadly Sins.* He is also the author of the horror, drama, *Paint the Silence,* and the modern day erotic love story, *Jagger's Revolution.*

Before writing books and stories, Kevin started out in the entertainment business in 1996 becoming actress Michelle Pfeiffer's personal development dude for her boutique production company, Via Rosa Productions. She dissolved her company after several years and he made a move into coordinating film productions for the big studios on such films as *One Fine Day, A Thousand Acres, The Deep End of the Ocean, Crazy in Alabama, Original Sin, The Perfect Storm, Harry Potter & the Sorcerer's Stone, Dr. Dolittle 2* and *Carolina.* He considers himself a beach bum born and raised in Los Angeles, California.

For more information, www.kevin-hunter.com